The Fine Art of

MARQUETRY

CREATING IMAGES IN WOOD
USING SAWN VENEERS

Craig Vandall Stevens

Schiffer Publishing Ltd

4880 Lower Valley Road · Atglen, Pennsylvania 19310

Other Schiffer Books By The Author:
The Art of Marquetry, 978-0-7643-0237-X, $16.95
Creating Coffee Tables: An Artistic Approach, 978-0-7643-0623-5, $29.95

Other Schiffer Books on Related Subjects:
Lighted Scroll Saw Projects, 978-0-7643-3386-6, $24.99

Schiffer Books are available at special discounts for bulk purchases for sales promotions or premiums. Special editions, including personalized covers, corporate imprints, and excerpts can be created in large quantities for special needs. For more information contact the publisher:

Published by Schiffer Publishing Ltd.
4880 Lower Valley Road
Atglen, PA 19310
Phone: (610) 593-1777; Fax: (610) 593-2002
E-mail: Info@schifferbooks.com

For the largest selection of fine reference books on this and related subjects, please visit our web site
at **www.schifferbooks.com**
We are always looking for people to write books on new and related subjects. If you have an idea for a book please contact us at the above address.

This book may be purchased from the publisher.
Include $5.00 for shipping.
Please try your bookstore first.
You may write for a free catalog.

In Europe, Schiffer books are distributed by
Bushwood Books
6 Marksbury Ave.
Kew Gardens
Surrey TW9 4JF England
Phone: 44 (0) 20 8392 8585; Fax: 44 (0) 20 8392 9876
E-mail: info@bushwoodbooks.co.uk
Website: www.bushwoodbooks.co.uk

Designed by RoS
Type set in Minion Pro/Korinna BT
ISBN: 978-0-7643-3499-3

Printed in China

DEDICATION

For my mom, Patty, thanks for the ginger-bread recipe....and everything else.

CONTENTS

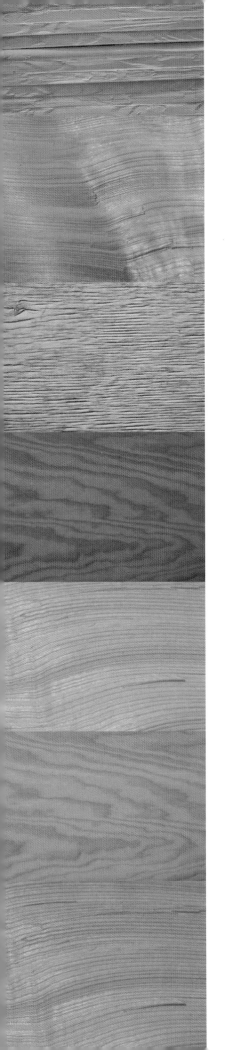

INTRODUCTION

In the early 1990s I had the incredible opportunity to study furniture making at the College of the Redwoods Fine Woodworking Program in northern California. The experience there was truly life changing, both as a person and as a craftsman. The College of the Redwoods Fine Woodworking Program has become synonymous with the highest level of craftsmanship in wood and the greatest attention to detail. I longed for those qualities in my own work—or in the work I imagined I would someday make. The program was a perfect fit for me, an environment in which I felt I began to thrive as a woodworker.

While there, I had the opportunity to see the work of many past students, some of which included the art of marquetry, and all of which were exquisitely made. The marquetry work caught my imagination, connecting with my natural interest in drawing and my art school background. Through trial and error, I developed a technique that worked well with the traditional double-bevel marquetry method and the thicker, hand-sawn veneers that we made at College of the Redwoods.

Now I make my living as a furniture craftsman, making one-of-a-kind furniture. The work is very satisfying and wonderfully time consuming. I work hard to honor the furniture making traditions and skills I learned as a student, and the ones I've learned in my own studio. Marquetry is a technique I often employ in my commissions and gallery pieces, always being careful to use the art form when it enhances a piece of furniture, but also being aware that not every furniture piece needs marquetry to be successful.

Marquetry is a technique used to create an image using the natural colors and patterns of wood. This book will focus on the double-bevel method of marquetry, a traditional technique that allows for a very precise fit of the individual pieces.

The double-bevel technique is ideal for creating a single, precisely fitting marquetry design. Its limitation is that, because the work is cut at an angle, only one piece can be made at a time. There are other marquetry methods that can make multiples of the same image, but those methods don't lend themselves to the really perfect fit that I'm aiming for in my own work.

The double-bevel method works with thick or thin veneers. When working with thin commercial veneers, the cutting angle increases to around 13 to 18 degrees, depending on the thickness of the veneer.

In this book, I'll focus on making marquetry by hand using a fret saw. I've chosen to demonstrate this method for several reasons, primarily because there is complete control over the speed and nuance of sawing. Along with being inexpensive, the 11" depth of the saw is large enough for doing many marquetry projects that are about jewelry box size. I feel strongly that using the fret saw greatly improves hand skills. The tool can truly begin to feel like an extension of the hand and offers very precise control. While it may feel awkward at the beginning, it can be easily mastered with practice.

The double-bevel technique works equally well using a variable speed scroll saw. Variable speed allows the motor to be slowed down for a more controlled cut. A scroll saw has the advantage of a deep throat, making it possible to work on larger projects. After learning marquetry by hand, it's very easy to then switch to a scroll saw when needed.

This book covers the basics of double-bevel marquetry with small practice projects. Then I'll demonstrate how to make a small marquetry panel, glued to a plywood core and edge banded. And in the last part of the book, there is a more challenging marquetry piece with sand shading and step-by-step design and construction of a small box.

I've had the great opportunity to teach many marquetry and furniture making classes at some of the best art centers and furniture making schools in North America. I welcome you to investigate some of these fine programs and learn about the classes they offer. I occasionally offer small or one-on-one workshops in my own studio. You can contact me or visit my website for upcoming schedules and workshop opportunities: http://www.cvstevens.com/.

ALSO, I sell packets of sawn veneers from my own inventory for folks that don't have the equipment or time to make their own. Feel free to contact me if you need an assortment of veneers to get started or would like to add to your supply of colors and textures.

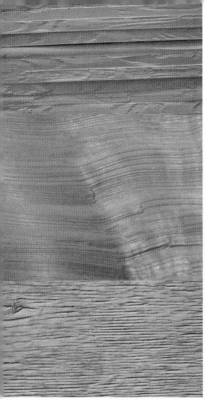

A WORD ABOUT VENEER

Veneer is a thin layer of wood that is applied to both sides of a core. Usually the core is high quality plywood, medium-density fiberboard (MDF), or other similar man-made material. Veneer can be very thin, such as commercially cut veneer, or thicker sawn veneer that can easily be made in a home woodworking shop. Commercial veneers range in thickness from about 1/30" to 1/40". Sawn veneer is usually 1/16" to something less than 1/8". I find a thickness of about 1/16" to be ideal. This thickness is easy to make and work with and it behaves like veneer, which means it doesn't expand and contract like solid wood. The thicker veneers can be finished with hand tools, just like solid wood, and a single board can yield many veneers. Precious material can be stretched very far using veneer.

Choosing Wood for Marquetry

There are several things to consider when selecting wood for use in marquetry. I believe some of the most successful marquetry designs are the result of careful attention to wood color, grain pattern, and texture, as well as a pleasing original drawing.

Creating the illusion of depth can be accomplished by combining wood species that have subtle variations in color, or by shading the wood with hot sand. Both methods can fool the eye into seeing three dimensions. With this in mind, it's very helpful to gather wood colors that have slightly different variations of light brown, dark brown, etc. A wide assortment of colors really extends your palette when shading with different species.

Sand shading is a method of creating the feeling of shadow in a marquetry design. Individual pieces of veneer are placed in hot sand for a short time to toast the wood. With just the right touch, this is a very effective technique for creating the illusion that the marquetry pieces are layered, or that one piece seems slightly behind another. However, it's easy to shade too much, which makes the piece much too dark and charred. A little sand shading goes a long way. After all, we're hoping someone viewing the finished piece is looking at the overall marquetry image and not distracted by individual pieces of wood that are too dark and burnt.

To my eye, the most successful sand shading is barely noticeable, giving the marquetry subject a nice, subtle sense of depth.

Finally, I would like to mention colorfastness. Many wood species become a nice, deeper version of their original color over time. Others begin to change in only a few hours and may turn out quite differently than planned. It's good to keep this in mind as you plan your projects.

American cherry is a good example of a wood that can change quickly, with the color deepening in a short period of time. Other woods like Osage orange or padauk change color pretty dramatically over time. I mention this because if Osage orange (bright yellow when freshly sawn) is chosen to make yellow marquetry flowers, eventually those flowers will become a warm brown. Becoming familiar with the tendencies of many different wood species can take some time, but it is an essential component to creating high quality marquetry.

So many colors and so little time! As I mentioned in the introduction, I make and use sawn veneers in my own work. There are several reasons I choose this method rather than using thin, commercial veneers.

• I want to treat the veneered surface as solid wood, meaning I prefer to use hand tools throughout the process of making a piece of furniture. Sawn veneers are approximately 1/16" thick (about 1.5mm), thick enough to hand plane or sand without the danger of going through the wood and revealing the plywood core. The 1/16" veneers are also very strong and easy to make and work with.

• The veneers and the solid wood parts of a furniture piece can be made from the same plank. For example, if I'm making a table, the veneers for the tabletop can be sawn from the same plank used to make the legs and rails. The color and grain match perfectly, as opposed to using commercial veneer for the tabletop and solid wood from a completely different plank for the rest of the table.

• Making your own veneers can really stretch the amount of wood used in a furniture or woodworking project. It's easy to get 10, or even 12, very good veneers from a 2" thick piece of wood. Again, using a small table as an example, one piece of 8/4 (2" thick) wood can make the table top surface as well as the underside of the table top. The grain pattern and color will match perfectly because all the wood came from the same part of the plank. It's a very ecological and efficient way of using wood. With any veneer work, it's important that both sides of a panel are veneered. This keeps the panel balanced. There is never a situation where veneer is applied to only one side of a plywood core.

Left to right: American elm, white oak, California oak, Japanese white oak, red oak, poplar, hickory, black walnut (air-dried), hard maple, beech, gray elm, curly ash, and birch

Left to right: Red gum, alder, red gum (pale), cherry, cherry (darker), European elm, European pear (steamed), and European pear (un-steamed)

Left to right: Soft woods—Alaskan yellow cedar, redwood (salvaged from a wine barrel), clear white pine, English yew, Douglas fir, and redwood (salvaged firewood)

Left to right: Ecologically harvested species—guatambu, narra (red color), arariba, t'zalam, kwila, and narra (gold color)

Left to right: apple, English brown oak, koa, bradford pear (domestic), spalted something (probably hickory*), English walnut, and European hornbeam *NOTE: It's common to have pieces of wood that are an unknown species.

Left to right: holly, apricot, bay laurel, black locust, harewood, and Russian olive

Left to right: imbuia, lacewood, imbuia (dark), jatoba, granadillo, and machiche

Left to right: Subtleness—birch, redwood, Douglas fir, European hornbeam, and English yew

Most marquetry designs are made up of several individual pieces of wood, assembled together to create a larger pattern. Most of the pieces are fairly small, the largest often being only a little larger than a coin.

With that small size in mind, the grain pattern and texture of the wood chosen for the marquetry pieces becomes very important. A curved pattern in the wood grain can help suggest a curved area in the design. In other words, the grain pattern can help fool the eye into seeing a curve in the design.

A straight grain pattern chosen for the same area can work against the design and make the image look very flat.

Here are two very different grain patterns, each useful in different ways. The redwood on top has subtle, curving grain on the left side and a tight, circular grain pattern near the middle. As you'll see later in the book, this type of pattern is very useful in marquetry. The straight grain of the Douglas fir below is also useful. When choosing wood, it's helpful to imagine the effect the grain pattern will have on the design. It can really help make marquetry come alive.

Left to right: red gum, American elm, harewood, English Yew, and European hornbeam

The textures and grain patterns shown in these veneers are very useful in creating a marquetry image that looks natural. They offer many choices for suggesting a shape or pattern within the design. Often these grain patterns are near knots, branches, or damaged areas of the tree.

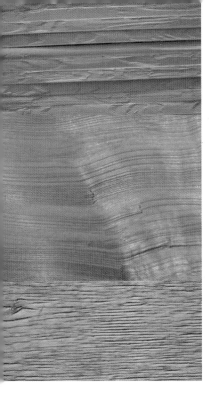

RE-SAWING VENEERS

I use a band saw to make my veneers. It's a very safe and efficient way of sawing veneers, and depending on the size of the band saw, you can make very wide veneers.

My band saw is a large, 36" saw that stands about 8' high. I saw a lot of veneers for the furniture and marquetry that I make in my shop, so the extra capacity and heavy-duty construction of the 1940s era saw are a real benefit to me. I'm often using the saw all day long and I get consistent, predictable results.

I use a 1" wide, carbide-tipped blade with about three teeth per inch. For smaller saws, a 1/2" wide carbon steel or bi-metal blade with three to four hook-shaped teeth per inch works very well.

Tuning Up a Band Saw

You can make a couple of different adjustments that help a band saw cut smoothly. The adjustments involve the guide blocks (or bearings) that sandwich the blade (indicated in the photo) and the thrust bearing that sits behind the blade. In the photo, the thrust bearing is the large bearing to the left and behind the blade. There are guide blocks and thrust bearings above and below the table. Each of them needs to be adjusted.

Before adjusting the blocks and bearings, I first make the tension of the blade very tight. The blade can handle the stress and I've found the saw generally behaves better with a lot of tension.

Next, I loosen the thrust bearings and move them away from the blade a little. I rotate the band saw wheels a little by hand so that I know the blade is centered on the tires. Then, I adjust the guide block so they are nearly touching the blade. I can just slide a piece of paper between each block and the blade. I do this above and below the table.

Then, I bring the thrust bearings, above and below the table, in very light contact with the back of the blade. I rotate the band saw wheels by hand to make sure the thrust bearing isn't contacting the blade too firmly. Once these adjustments are made, I check that everything is tightened and turn on the saw. When the saw is up to speed, I look at the relationship of the blocks and bearings. The thrust bearings are lightly spinning while the saw is running (and not cutting wood), but not under great pressure from the blade.

The next important step for re-sawing veneers successfully is setting the "drift" of the blade. This is the direction or angle that each blade wants to cut naturally. Whenever I put a new blade on the saw, I recheck the drift before sawing. I determine the drift of the blade with a piece of thick, straight scrap wood that is a couple of feet long. I draw a line parallel to a straight edge of the wood.

Then, with the saw running, I begin cutting on the pencil line. I try to cut very accurately, pushing only from the back of the wood, in other words, pushing the pencil line. My other hand only applies enough downward pressure to keep the wood from bouncing. My pushing hand has to make small adjustments left and right to keep the blade following the line.

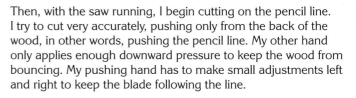

Once I've cut about half the length of the board, I hold it down on the band saw table and turn off the saw. When the saw has come to a stop, I hold an adjustable bevel square against the edge of the table with the blade against the wood. This angle is the drift of the blade. I tighten the bevel square and refer to it any time I need to set the band saw fence.

This is my shop-made band saw fence. It's about 5" tall and very square.

Raise the guide assembly above the fence.

Set the distance between the fence and the blade tooth to 3/32". This distance will give me a cut that is a little thicker than my final veneer thickness, which is 5/64".

I ALWAYS work with a veneer thickness of 5/64". At the end of a project, after the marquetry work is finished and the veneers have been scraped and sanded, the final thickness will be about 1/16". This thickness works very well for furniture and it won't expand and contract once it's glued to a plywood core.

TIP

I check the drift angle, and then recheck the distance between the fence and the blade.

Then clamp the fence to the table, front and back.

I turn on the saw and make a cut about 3/8" long on a scrap of wood...

Then, I hold the scrap near the top of the fence and cut along the kerf I just made. This tells me if the fence is truly parallel to the blade. If the second cut contacts the wood a little, rather than following perfectly in the kerf, I need to change the tilt of the table a little.

I'll make veneers from this 2" thick piece of sycamore. I've jointed one face of the board and jointed one edge square to the face. Before I make any cuts, I draw a cabinetmaker's triangle on the end of the board. This allows me to reassemble the veneers in the order they grew. This is especially helpful for book-matching veneers.

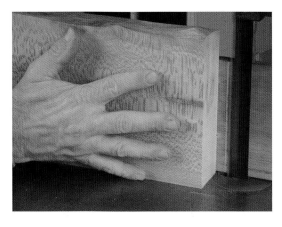

With the saw running, I hold the jointed face against the fence and begin the cut. My left hand is pushing forward, while my right hand applies constant pressure against the fence.

Another view as I begin the cut. I keep a steady feed rate once I begin cutting. This assures a very flat, consistent veneer.

As I approach the end of the board, I use a push stick to feed the last few inches. My right hand continues to apply a little forward pressure as I reach for the push stick.

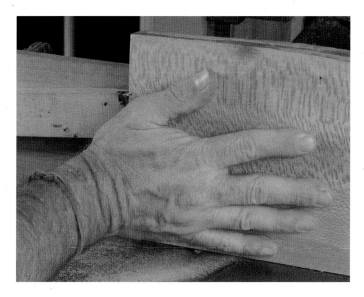

The last couple of inches.

A finished 3/32" veneer. The remaining sycamore board can be re-jointed now or, if the surface is smooth, I can begin cutting the next veneer without jointing.

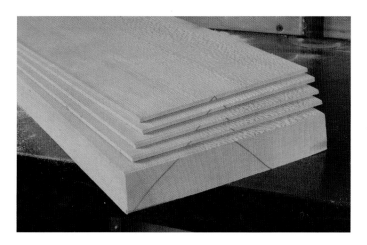

Four sawn veneers. It's easy to see the advantage of having the cabinetmaker's triangle on the board before re-sawing. It makes it very easy to reorganize the veneers later.

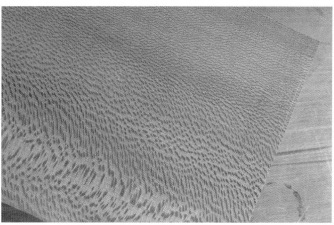

The unusual pattern of quarter-sawn sycamore is very versatile for marquetry.

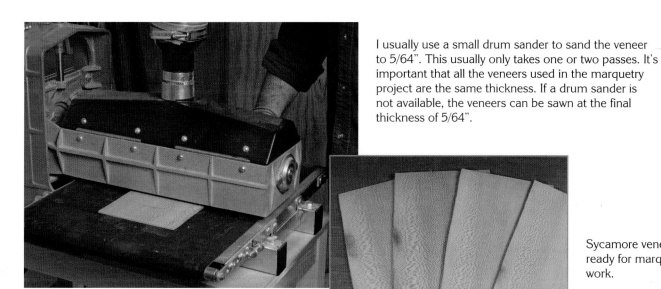

I usually use a small drum sander to sand the veneer to 5/64". This usually only takes one or two passes. It's important that all the veneers used in the marquetry project are the same thickness. If a drum sander is not available, the veneers can be sawn at the final thickness of 5/64".

Sycamore veneers ready for marquetry work.

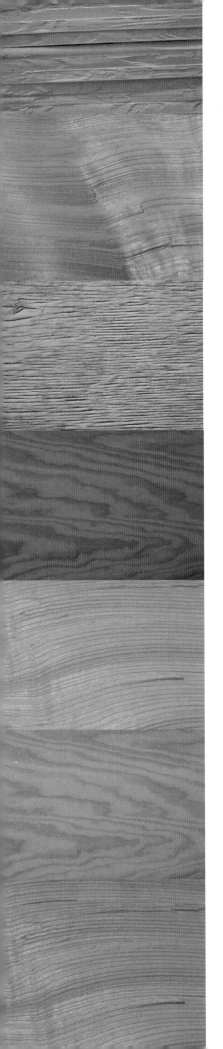

THE MARQUETRY TOOL KIT

The tools needed for doing double-bevel marquetry by hand are (*opposite, top: clockwise, from top right*) deep throat fret saw, regular masking tape, accordion glue bottle with yellow or white woodworker's glue, small hammer, stylus, hand scraper, #69 drill bits, package of 2/0 jeweler's blades, pin vise (2), small counter-sink (seen mounted in one of the pin vises), loose 2/0 jeweler's saw blades, and a wooden sawing table, called a donkey. See the patterns section in the back of the book for a scale drawing of a donkey.

Sources for these tools are found at the back of the book.

• Regarding the glue, it's best to use regular woodworker's glue rather than the quicker setting water-resistant glues.

• A fret saw accepts flat, jeweler's blades (not to be confused with a coping saw).

• Fret saw blades, also called jewelers blades, are available in a wide range of sizes. The 2/0 size blades are strong and can cut intricate shapes. They're sold by the dozen or by the gross.

• The countersinks I use are actually carving burrs for a Dremel Moto Tool.

• A donkey is a small, wooden cutting table with a "V"-shaped notch or bird's mouth. The sawing is done in the bird's mouth area. The marquetry donkey I use is adjustable, so that the cutting angle can be changed for working with thick or thin veneers. However, a fixed-angle donkey works great and is a little easier to make.

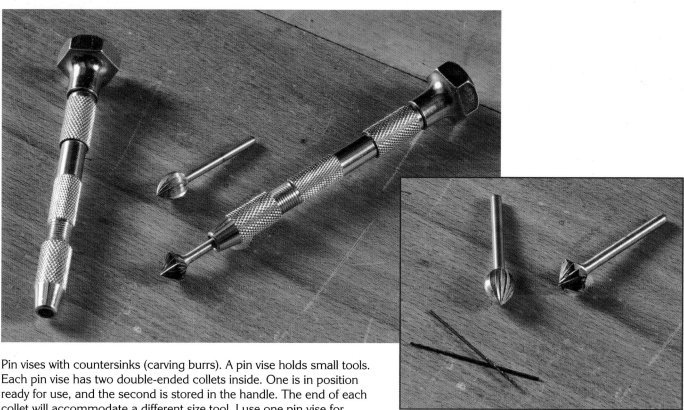

Pin vises with countersinks (carving burrs). A pin vise holds small tools. Each pin vise has two double-ended collets inside. One is in position ready for use, and the second is stored in the handle. The end of each collet will accommodate a different size tool. I use one pin vise for holding the small #69 drill bit and the second for a small countersink. The countersink is only occasionally needed for fret saw work. It's more helpful when cutting marquetry with a scroll saw.

Countersinks and #69 drill bits. The drill bits are used for piercing the veneers so the saw blade can be threaded. Countersinks are available in different shapes (carving burrs), all of which work well.

Double-Bevel Marquetry Techniques

The first exercise will help you develop a feel for the double-bevel sawing technique and dial-in the sawing angle. Begin with a small piece of light colored veneer and draw a simple shape at one edge. The veneer I've chosen is alder. Make the shape big enough to handle easily, about the size of a small coin. This exercise is a great way to practice sawing while chasing a perfect fit.

It's important that the shape be a little narrower at the edge of the veneer so that you can get an accurate test fit. A shape that is wider at the edge isn't as helpful when trying to determine if the sawing was done at the correct angle.

Tape the light colored alder veneer to a darker veneer of similar size, aligning an edge and an end. Tape tightly so that the veneers can't slip. The darker veneer is walnut.

Taped and ready to go.

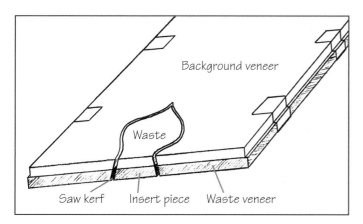

Background veneer

Waste

Saw kerf   Insert piece   Waste veneer

Before

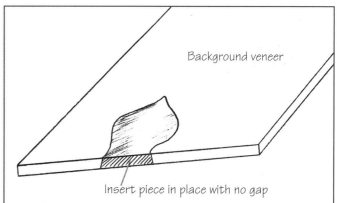

Background veneer

Insert piece in place with no gap

After

Fret saws have a small finger-like tab on the frame. The tab allows the saw to be hung on the edge of a bench or the donkey, freeing a hand to attach the blade.

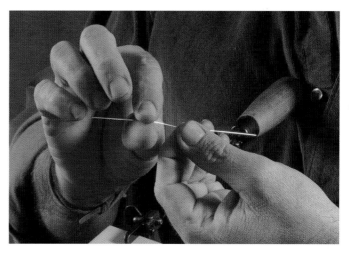

While supporting the saw with your chest or shoulder, find the blades tooth direction. The blade should be attached with the teeth facing away from the saw frame and the teeth should be pointed toward the handle (in this photo, the teeth are pointed toward the ceiling). The saw cuts on the down stroke. The teeth are difficult to see, but easily felt.

With the saw tab hanging on the donkey, place the end of the blade in the handle clamp and tighten. Both hands are free to do this.

Use your chest or shoulder to push the saw handle toward the donkey. I push until the saw frame is flexed enough to place the blade all the way in the top clamp and tighten. The saw will cut better if the blade is under full tension, so be sure to flex the saw until the blade goes completely in the top clamp.

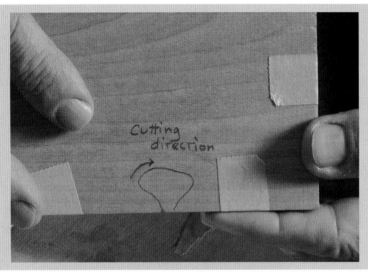

Now, make the first practice cut. It's very important to cut in the correct direction. If you saw the wrong way around the shape, the piece will be much too small. Cut clockwise around the shape, as seen in the photograph. Because the donkey is tilted at an angle, cutting in a clockwise direction creates a tight fit when the piece from the bottom veneer is placed in the opening of the background veneer.

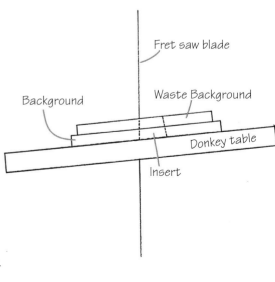

Ready to begin sawing. This is a good time to talk about the most important skill to develop for cutting marquetry by hand. The saw frame needs to be held completely vertical—truly 90° from the top of the workbench.

The donkey is angled at about 8°. So it's important to saw as close to vertical as possible to maintain the 8° bevel cut.

Being right-handed, I find it comfortable to position myself so tha. my right eye is lined up with the center of the donkey.

Begin with the practice veneers located near the narrow part of the bird's mouth. Because the saw teeth are facing away from the saw frame and down toward the handle, the cutting action will cut forward and keep the work piece firmly on the donkey. If the work piece wants to keep lifting off the donkey, check that the teeth are not upside down (lifting the veneers).

The fingers of my left hand control the work piece, rotating it to allow the blade to follow the cutting line. The saw only travels up and down, like a sewing machine. Try to keep the saw lined up and parallel with the donkey. My left hand does all the turning. Begin cutting with some short strokes until the blade is moving easily.

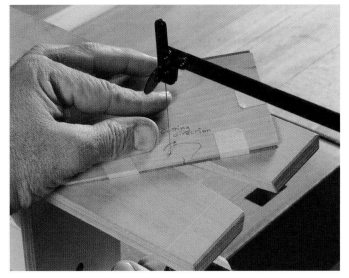

The goal of these practice pieces is to learn to saw straight up and down. It's not really important at this stage to worry about following the pencil line perfectly. Try to be more aware of the saw and less focused on the line. With the blade about 1/4" into the cut, my left hand begins to slowly rotate the work piece.

Stop the sawing motion once in a while to check the angle of the saw. If you've left the vertical position, adjust the saw and keep cutting.

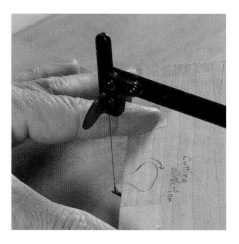

I am halfway through the shape. Again, I'm constantly glancing at the saw to keep it vertical.

As the blade nears the end of the cut, slide the work piece to the right a little so the blade is near the donkey. This will prevent the small pieces from falling through the bird's mouth.

The completed cut.

The alder veneer is on top. Again, this is actually called the background veneer (the pattern is always drawn on the background veneer). The small, cutout alder piece on top is the waste piece and can be discarded. The small walnut piece below is the insert piece.

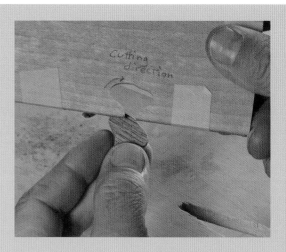

The walnut insert piece is ready for a test fit.

Turn the work piece and the insert piece over and press the insert piece into place. You can tap it lightly with a small hammer if necessary. Now we see the advantage of having these practice veneers taped together with the edges even. The insert piece can be fit into place without un-taping the veneers. Many test pieces can be cut along the edges as you perfect your sawing motion. This is very helpful because it usually takes several practice cuts to achieve a nice fit.

A nice, tight fit. The insert piece is perfectly flush with the background veneer. You can consistently accomplish this kind of fit if the angle of the donkey is correct and the saw travels vertically throughout the cut. Normally at this stage, the insert piece can be glued into place. Gluing will be discussed later. For now, the piece can be left in place or set aside.

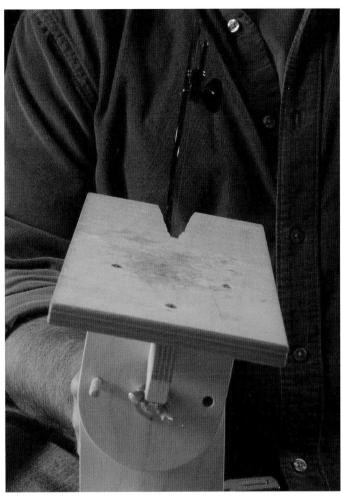

On this second test piece, I'll cut with the saw less than vertical, in other words, lessening the angle. This will demonstrate the problems that occur when the saw is not vertical. Here's a new shape drawn beside the first.

A head-on view of the saw, held at an angle. I'm exaggerating the error a little for the photograph. This is a common problem most people experience when first beginning. By not holding the saw 90° to the bench top, the bevel angle quickly becomes less than 8°. The result is a loose fitting insert piece. The saw may be cutting at 5° or 6°, so the insert piece may fall completely through the background veneer.

The second test piece is cut just like the first, clockwise around the shape. Sawing near the narrow section of the bird's mouth, my left hand rotates the work piece. Again, I'm exaggerating the angle to help demonstrate.

Halfway around the shape.

Completing the cut. I've moved the work piece to the right side of the bird's mouth (my right side) to prevent the pieces from falling. I'm holding the pieces with my index finger as I finish the cut.

Removing the saw.

The small, alder waste piece can be discarded.

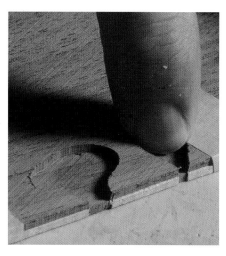

Turn the work piece and the insert piece over and press the insert piece into place.

Loose fit. The insert piece pushes nearly all the way through the background veneer. The cutting angle was so much less than vertical, which gave the insert piece a small gap around its perimeter and created a loose fit.

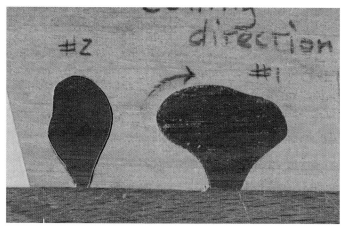

Detail showing the difference between the two pieces. When piece #2 is flush with the background veneer, we can see the gap. The goal is to have a wood-to-wood fit. Glue won't bridge the gap and the piece doesn't look good.

Tips for Sawing Correctly

KEEPING the fret saw moving vertical is the key to a nice fit. This takes some practice. If the pieces don't fit tightly, keep at it and try to focus on the saw stroke. It does get easier with practice and soon it will be second nature.

• Try lining the center of the donkey with your shoulder (right shoulder if you're right handed). If you're sawing from the center of your body, it's a little more difficult to move straight up and down.

• Try exaggerating a vertical stroke by sawing a little greater than vertical—as though you are sawing at 9°. Usually this little correction is enough to get a perfect fit.

• I've noticed that for most people the fit improves after taking a break. Tomorrow your marquetry is going to be much nicer and the day after tomorrow it's going to be amazing!

Turn the work piece over.

And press the insert piece into place.

The piece might need a slight hammer tap to make it flush with the background veneer.

Glued in place and ready to move on.

I've discarded the piece that didn't fit, and now I'll keep working my way around the practice work piece. Reposition the veneers as necessary, keeping in mind that the walnut veneer below is getting pretty cut up. If repositioning the veneers, make sure there's wood below before you make your practice cuts. Follow the same steps to make one practice piece after another until the basic technique feels comfortable and the insert pieces fit.

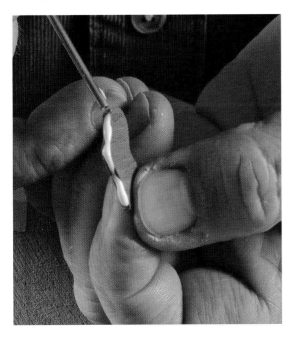

As the pieces are beginning to fit better, it's time to get a feel for gluing them into the background veneers. After testing the fit, remove the insert piece and apply a small amount of glue around the edge with the accordion glue bottle.

Now it's time to practice cutting sharp corners. On the background veneer, draw a shape that has two or three sharp corners. Reposition the veneers if necessary.

Begin sawing as before, keeping the saw frame vertical.

As the blade reaches the first corner, I stop the forward pressure. Begin slowly turning the work piece while moving the saw up and down—but not pushing forward. After turning the work piece a little, I begin pulling the saw back toward myself a little. The idea is to pivot at the corner until the saw is lined up with the new direction. Then begin cutting forward again.

Beginning to rotate the work piece and pulling back slightly on the saw. Pivoting.

The work piece is now turned so the blade is lined up with the new direction. Now I begin cutting forward again.

At the next corner, repeat the pivoting technique. Stop the forward pressure and slowly begin turning the work piece. This corner is a little sharper, so I'll be pivoting a little longer. I pull back slightly on the saw after the work piece begins turning.

TIP

WHEN the blade reaches the corner, push the saw handle forward, farther under the donkey. This helps assure the insert piece below has a nice, long point.

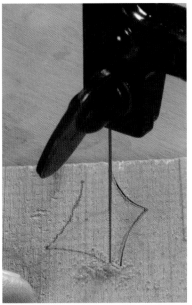

Now, begin moving forward again, cutting a nice curve to the next corner.

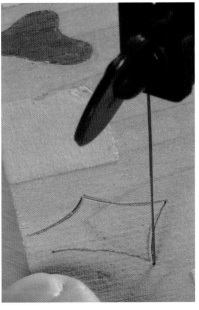

And repeat again. Stop your forward pressure, push the handle forward slightly, and begin rotating the work piece while moving the saw up and down. Then begin moving forward again.

Insert and waste piece removed.

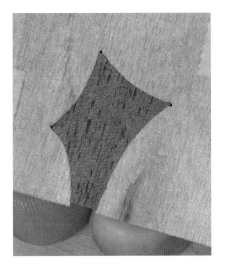

The insert piece pressed into place. Notice the tiny holes in the corners. The 2/0 saw blade has a rectangular profile. In order to turn the corner, the teeth need to clear a small path as the blade pivots. These tiny holes are the result of the blade turning on itself.

TIP

AS A MARQUETRY project nears completion, scraping and sanding will help the tiny holes disappear. This space can be minimized by pushing the saw handle forward, farther under the donkey as the saw turns the corner. Once you're past the corner, return the saw handle to it's normal straight up and down position.

Working in the Middle of the Veneer

The next step is to leave the veneer edges and put a marquetry piece in the middle of the veneer. Sawing from the edge is a great way to get a feel for the sawing stroke and understand the double-bevel technique. However, in actual practice, all marquetry is usually done inside the edge of the background veneer. So, the next step is to learn to pierce, or thread, the blade through the veneer. This method allows you to begin sawing anywhere in the design you choose.

I'll begin working with a new pair of veneers. My background veneer is cherry and the bottom veneer will be walnut.

Before I begin working again, I'll clean the surface of the donkey. I often glue the marquetry pieces in place on top of the donkey, so over time the glue builds up and the work piece doesn't move as easily over the surface. I use a sharpened card scraper to remove the dried glue.

Tape the veneers together with four or five pieces of masking tape. This time, tape the veneers together at an angle to each other.

I'll put a couple of pieces of masking tape on the backside. I don't want to use more tape than necessary, but I want to use enough tape to keep the veneers from slipping.

Again, the cherry veneer is the background veneer. Draw a new simple shape on the background veneer. I double-check to make sure there is wood below the new shape!

Now we can begin using one of the pin vises. The pin vise contains two collets. One collet is in the nose and the other is stored in the handle. Each collet has two ends. So, with one pin vise you can hold a wide range of tools, such as drill bits. Look for the smallest collet opening. This is the one we'll be using for the #69 drill.

Reassemble the pin vise with the smallest collet end facing the tip of the tool. Insert the #69 drill bit into the collet. These small drill bits are very fragile. You only need about a 1/4" of the bit to extend beyond the collet—just enough to drill through two pieces of veneer. Tighten the collet fairly tight.

This is the position for using the pin vise. The index finger rests on the back of the pin vise, applying downward pressure. The back of the handle (the part contacting the index finger) pivots freely, making it very easy for the other fingers and thumb to rotate the tool.

The location of the hole is very important. I'll be sawing again in a clockwise direction. I locate the drill hole on the left side of the shape (as I'm looking at it). I think of this as the downhill side of the shape, because as I'm looking at the work piece, the left side of the drawing is lower than the right side since the donkey is tilted at an angle. It's very important to remember this. Drilling the hole in the correct location puts me in position to saw properly in a clockwise direction.

This is a good location for the hole. It's an easy place to begin sawing and it's also easy to finish sawing when I've worked around the shape. I want to avoid drilling the hole near a corner or in a location that is a little difficult. This location makes it as easy as possible.

Rotate the pin vise while the applying some downward pressure with your index finger. I'm careful to keep the pin vise straight. The small drill bit is very fragile and can break easily. I'm especially careful when removing the drill after the hole is finished.

This view from the backside of the bench shows the vertical position of the pin vise. This ensures that the hole is drilled at the same 8° angle we'll be sawing at.

I've moved the work piece to my left so I don't drill into the donkey. I'm rotating the pin vise clockwise, slowly drilling through the two veneers. As I begin to drill through the bottom piece, I hold my finger below the drill bit so I can feel it come through. Then, I continue rotating clockwise as I pull the drill straight out of the hole. This removes any sawdust with the drill bit.

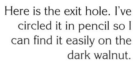

Here is the exit hole. I've circled it in pencil so I can find it easily on the dark walnut.

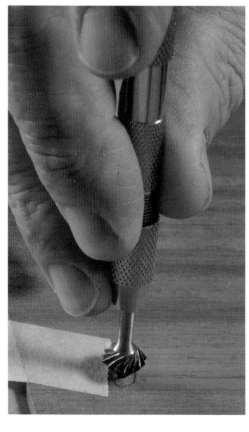

A couple of light twists with the pin vise is all that's needed to clean up any loose wood fibers.

I occasionally use the second pin vise with the countersink. Sometimes the drill will leave ragged wood fibers around the exit hole. The countersink cleans them up and also leaves a small, funnel-shaped opening in the hole.

I DON'T usually use the countersink when doing marquetry by hand with the fret saw and donkey. The countersink really helps when working with a scroll saw. If I'm using a scroll saw, I always countersink at this point because it's more difficult to thread the blade through the hole when using a scroll saw. The scroll saw table prevents seeing the hole clearly. By countersinking the opening, the blade threads more easily.

However, it's nice to have the countersink available if needed for hand-sawn marquetry as well.

TIP

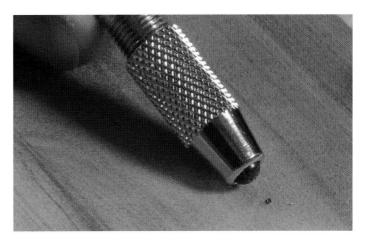

Before beginning the next practice piece, I'll address what to do if a drill bit gets broken off in the veneers. The drills are very brittle and at some point you'll run into this. I'll use a couple of veneer scraps to demonstrate. The drill bits break if they're flexed. It's really important to drill the hole and remove the drill with as little bending as possible. But they do however break sometimes. Here are a couple of ways to deal with broken pieces that remain in the work piece.

This is pretty typical. The drill bit broke flush with the top veneer and is protruding from the bottom veneer.

A small pair of needle-nose pliers can usually grab the small section of drill. Once removed you can go ahead and thread the blade through the hole and begin cutting.

However, sometimes the drill breaks off so close to both surfaces of the work piece that you can't grab it with pliers. If that's the case, it's easiest to un-tape the work piece and remove the broken piece of drill with the pliers. Then reposition the veneers so the hole in the bottom piece will be missed in the next cut and begin again.

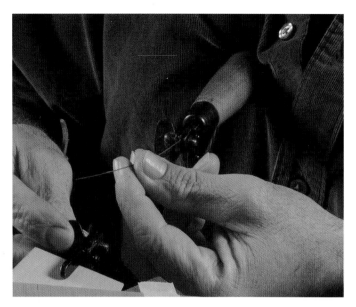

Back to the work piece: the chest or shoulder supports the fret saw while it hangs on the donkey. Release the top blade clamp.

Hold the loose end of the saw blade in one hand and the work piece in the other with the bottom veneer facing you.

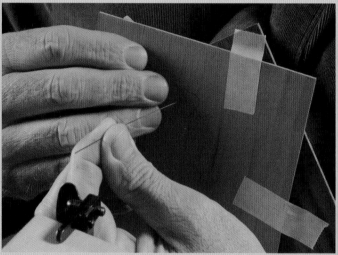

Thread the blade through the hole.

Carefully slide the work piece all the way to the handle of the fret saw.

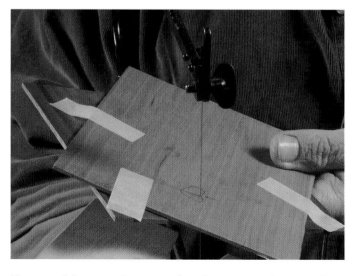

The work piece will support itself at the handle, freeing both hands to tighten the blade in the top clamp.

Now, carefully move the saw and work piece together onto the donkey for sawing.

Ready to begin cutting. It's easy to break the blade when moving the pair back to the donkey, so move carefully.

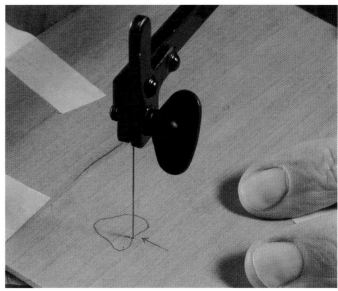

Remember the drill hole is located on the left side of the work piece, or the downhill side. Before you begin sawing, place the work piece in the same position it was in when drilling.

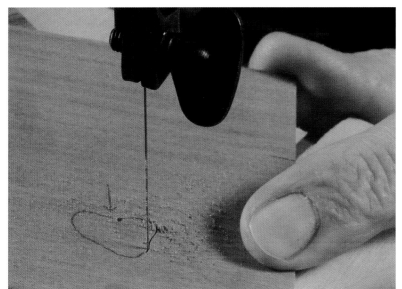

The sawing is the same as before. Keep the blade near the narrow part of the bird's mouth, hold the fret saw completely vertical, and saw around the shape. If the sawing becomes very difficult, it probably means you're sawing into the donkey. As you might imagine, sawing the donkey at the same time makes marquetry much more difficult. Don't do that.

The fret saw is lined up with my right eye and I'm sitting in a comfortable position. I'm taking smooth saw strokes and regularly glancing at the saw and my sawing hand to confirm that the stroke is vertical.

I OFTEN check my location in the bird's mouth by stopping the saw and sliding the work piece left and right to feel the bird's mouth with the saw blade. I then resume sawing.

TIP

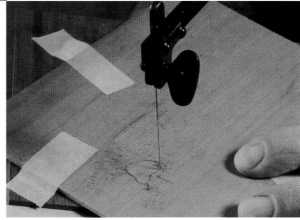

Working my way around the shape. As I approach the starting point, I want to line the saw up with the kerf created when I began cutting. This allows a smooth transition between the starting point and the finishing point, as opposed to a jagged, dogleg shape.

Just before I complete the cut, I move the work piece and saw to the right side of the bird's mouth so the cutout piece doesn't fall. Carefully take the last few saw strokes.

When the cut is complete, loosen the top clamp.

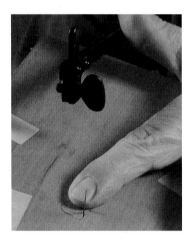  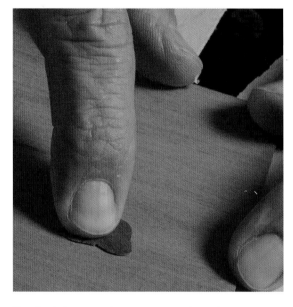

Pull the blade out of the work piece, holding the cutout pieces in place with a finger.

Remove the tape from the veneers.

Set the bottom walnut veneer aside and turn the background veneer over. Discard the small cherry waste piece and fit the walnut insert piece into the background veneer.

Turn the work piece over again and we can see a nice fit. Notice we can see some of the drill hole in the walnut. With the next piece, I'll introduce a small change we can make when drilling the hole that will eliminate this little hole. The fit is the result of sawing vertically and always being aware of the saw position. When working I split my attention equally between following the pencil line and the saw stroke.

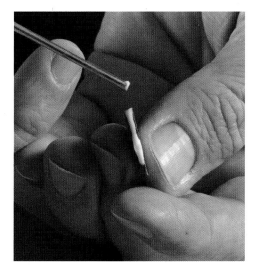

Use the accordion glue bottle to put a small amount of glue around the insert piece. The work piece is upside down on the donkey or bench.

Press the insert piece in place and tap lightly with a hammer to make sure it sits flush with the good side of the background veneer.

There's no need to allow the glue to dry before adding another piece. I even plan on cutting through the first insert piece to create a shape that overlaps with the first.

Tape a new veneer under the background veneer. This time I'm using a piece of white oak. Any grain direction is sufficient for this practice piece.

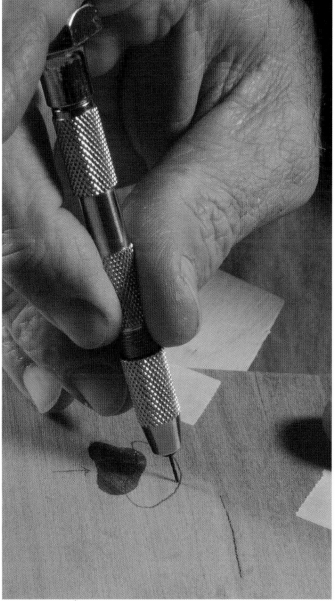

I'll change the drilling angle a little to prevent the drill hole from being seen when the piece is in place. I locate the drill hole in a place that will be easy to begin the first few saw strokes and also easy to complete the cut. In this simple, rounded shape, just about anywhere will do.

The hole left by the drill can be eliminated from the finished marquetry piece with a simple adjustment to the drilling angle. Rather than drilling vertical, tilt the pin vise a little past vertical. The donkey is angled at 8°—if the pin vise it tilted at 10° or 11°, the drill will enter the waste piece on top and exit the bottom veneer outside of the insert piece. This sounds much more confusing than it really is. With a little practice, you'll never see any indication of the drill hole.

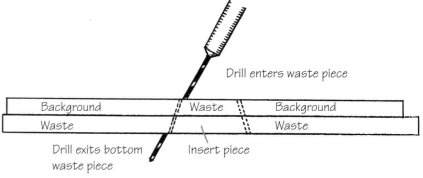

Drill enters waste piece

Background	Waste	Background
Waste		Waste

Drill exits bottom waste piece

Insert piece

Drilling at the exaggerated angle. The index finger applies a little downward pressure while the other the thumb and other fingers rotate the pin vise.

The hole is nice and clean. As is usually the case when cutting marquetry by hand, I won't use the countersink. I can see the hole clearly when lining up the blade.

Thread the blade through the hole as before. Support the fret saw with the shoulder and the saw's tab, insert the blade, and slide the work piece all the way down the blade to the handle.

Place the blade in the top clamp and tighten.

Hold the saw as vertical as possible and begin cutting around the shape. Use a steady stroke and rotate the work piece smoothly.

I HAVE a tip that will help make the transition from the beginning of the cut to the end of the cut very smooth. As I begin sawing, I hold the blade against the left side of the hole. The hole is small, but the saw blade is much smaller. If I keep the blade against the left side of the hole, and then aim at the left side of the hole when I finish the cut, I'll have a very fluid line. This will help assure there is no sign of the drill hole in the insert piece.

TIP

Nothing changes as you reach the previous insert piece. That first piece is now just a part of the background veneer.

As I approach the starting point, I'm looking closely at the kerf created as I began sawing. I'm not focusing on the pencil line any more, because the kerf is the real line now. I want to guide the blade to the hole in as smooth a line as possible.

Since I started the cut with the blade against the left side of the hole, I'm aiming at that spot now—even if I need to leave my pencil line to do so. A smooth kerf is much more important, because when the piece is glued into place, there will not be evidence of where the cut began and finished. In other words, when someone looks at the finished work, I want he or she to only see the marquetry image. I don't want any signs of the technique to be visible.

Remove the blade from the work piece.

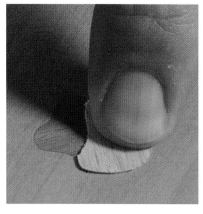

With the tape removed and the background veneer turned over, test the fit of the insert piece.

The fit is nice and the hole is not visible in the insert piece. Remove the piece, apply glue, and tap it into place.

Wiping off extra glue.

Now I'll add a third and final piece to the practice work piece. This is a piece of cypress with very straight grain. I've drawn a shape with points so we can practice cutting corners. I'll orient the grain of the cypress so that it runs with the long lines of the new shape. This is a chance to experiment with choosing grain and pattern as you're positioning the veneers together.

Tape the veneers together in the front and back, if necessary, to keep them from slipping.

I'll drill the hole for the cypress insert piece in the middle of one of the long lines of this shape. This location is easy to begin and finish sawing. I don't want the hole to be near a corner. I'm holding the drill at a steeper angle—10° or 11°—so the hole will be invisible in the insert piece. The practice work piece and first projects are good opportunities to get a feel for that angle.

The exit hole on the bottom veneer is a little fuzzy. This is common with some wood species, like cypress, which is a little difficult to thread the blade through.

The countersink cleans up the area around the hole.

Looking over my left shoulder: The fret saw is hanging from the donkey and supported by my shoulder. I am threading the blade through the work piece.

Slide the work piece all the way to the handle and tighten the top clamp. Be sure to push the blade as far into the clamp as possible.

Carefully rotate the saw and work piece into place on the donkey.

Position the blade near the back of the bird's mouth and hold the saw as vertical as possible. The saw is lined up to begin cutting along the pencil line.

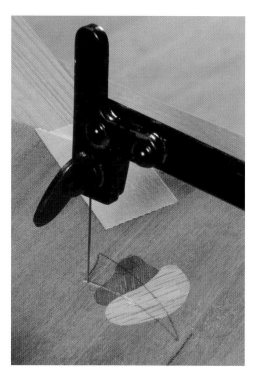

Follow the pencil line to the first corner. When I reach the corner, I push the handle a little forward toward the donkey and slowly begin to rotate the work piece, pulling back slightly on the saw.

After turning the corner, begin sawing forward again.

Repeat the process at the next corner. Remember to work slowly and focused. Corners will get much easier as you practice.

Sawing toward the last corner.

Ah! Broken blade. Sometimes one blade will last for a complete project and sometimes they'll break every few minutes. This is a good reason to buy them by the gross. It's very easy to replace the blade, even when it breaks in the middle of a cut.

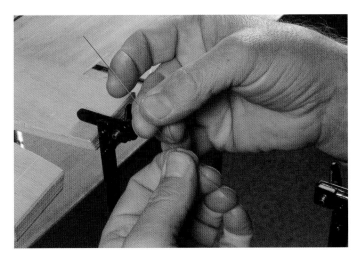

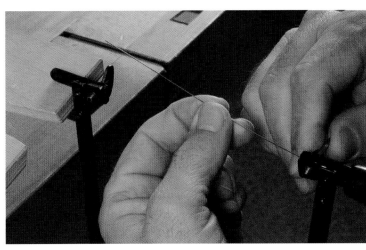

Remove the broken blade from the saw. There may be a small piece of blade stuck in the veneers. Pull it out with pliers.

Find the tooth direction with your fingers.

Tighten the blade in the handle clamp.

With the bottom veneer facing you, thread the blade through the saw kerf at the point where the blade broke.

Make sure the teeth are headed in the direction of the cut.

Slide the work piece all the way to the handle and tighten the top clamp.

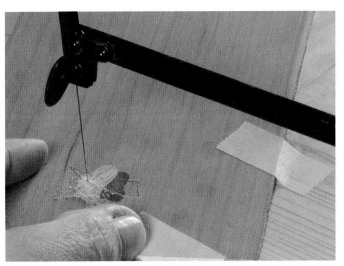

Carefully rotate the work piece and saw back into the cutting position. Ready to cut again.

I want to follow the pencil line, but always make sure the saw is vertical. Move smoothly through the other insert pieces.

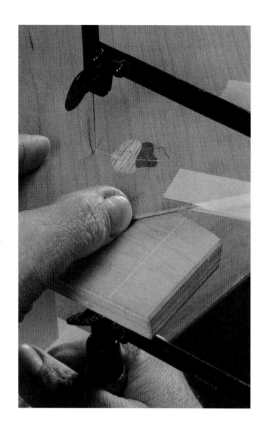

At the corner, slow down and push the saw handle forward toward the donkey. As soon as you begin to rotate the work piece, pull back slightly on the saw. Keep moving the saw up and down as you work your way around the corner.

When the saw is lined up with the pencil line again, begin cutting toward the drill hole.

When the blade is about 1/4" from the hole, I'm really focused on the saw kerf in front of the blade and the left side of the hole. This will give me a very smooth transition between the beginning and end of the cut. Slide the work piece to the right so the pieces don't fall through the bird's mouth.

With the cut complete, loosen the blade from the top clamp and slide the saw away from the work piece.

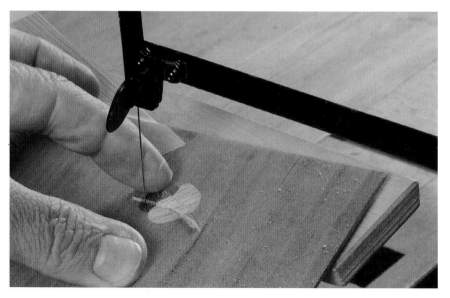

Remove the tape and set the waste piece and the bottom veneer aside.

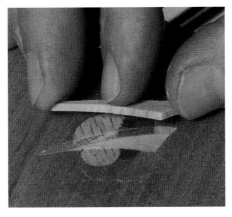

Turn the work piece over and test the insert piece.

The fit is perfect and it's ready to be glued in place.

Place a little glue along the edges of the cypress piece and press it into the backside of the background veneer.

I slide the work piece toward the back of the donkey so I'm tapping over the supported center. The front of the donkey is a little too flexible for tapping, especially if the fit of the piece is a little tight.

Here is the cypress piece glued in place.

For practice, keep building on these simple shapes and become more comfortable with the double-bevel technique. Practice all the steps and experiment with different shapes.

FIRST PROJECT

The first project is a simple leaf design made up of three pieces of wood. The leaf's center vein is a curving line. (The leaf pattern is located in the back of the book.)

While sketching, I'm keeping the leaf's proportions in mind. I want the visual weight of the leave's two halves to be balanced with the size of the stem.

Once the pencil sketch is finished, trace the design onto vellum or tracing paper.

The finished pattern.

Choose a piece of veneer for the project. I'll refer to this piece of wood as the background veneer. The pattern is always drawn on the background veneer. For this first practice project, choose a light colored veneer so the design is visible. This piece of soft maple measures about 6" x 5".

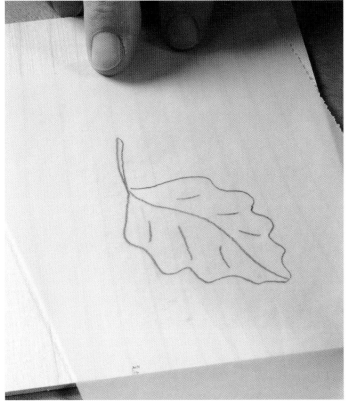

Place the pattern on the veneer. Although this is a very simple leaf design, it's an opportunity to think about composition. Move the pattern around on the veneer and consider a location other than the center. Positioning the leaf a little closer to the bottom and a little off-center can help suggest a little movement in the design, as though the leaf were falling. I've positioned the maple grain vertically. This can also help create the illusion of something moving from top to bottom.

On this small veneer, there's not a lot of room to really create the feeling of movement. However, being aware of composition is an interesting and important part of marquetry.

Once the pattern is in place, tape it in place at one edge. Transfer the sketch to the veneer with graphite paper. Graphite paper is available from art supply stores. It transfers a finer line than carbon paper and can be erased more easily. Place it between the pattern and the veneer with the dark side down.

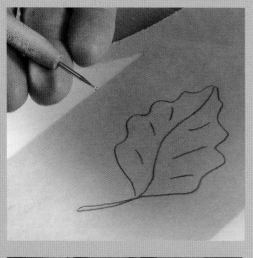

I use a stylus to transfer the image, rather than a pencil. The stylus leaves a very fine line while keeping the original pattern free of additional pencil lines. Styli are available in craft stores and art supply stores.

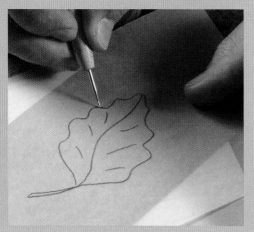

Trace all the pencil lines with the stylus.

Without removing the pattern, check that the complete pattern transferred.

While the pattern is still in place, draw a couple of marks on the vellum to help relocate the pattern later. Make sure these marks transfer.

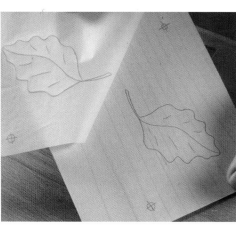

Remove the pattern.

The six short marks inside the leaf help visualize the grain direction of the veneer pieces that will be fit into the design.

Veneer Selection

Our first project is on a maple background. I've chosen two colors and patterns that not only go well together, but also look good on the maple. I am using Douglas fir (right) for the two halves of the leaf and English walnut (left) for the center vein.

English walnut is a little lighter in color than black walnut. It will be seen as a thin line, so if the color is too dark, it will look black. I want the center vein to stand out slightly from the two halves of the leaf, but I don't want it to call too much attention to itself. The very straight grain of the Douglas fir will help suggest the leaf's vein direction.

TIP

OVER THE YEARS, I have accumulated a large amount of wood, which when sawn into veneers makes for a really wide range of colors and patterns for marquetry. If you're just beginning to gather wood for marquetry, you may not have access to some of the woods I'm demonstrating with. Scrap pieces from just about any woodworking project are likely big enough to make a few veneers and can serve as the beginning of a nice collection.

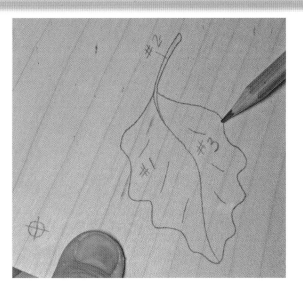

Here is the leaf drawing on the maple background. I'll number the pieces in a good cutting sequence. I'll begin with one of the halves (Douglas fir), then cut in the stem (English walnut), and end with the other half (Douglas fir). As the work progresses, you will see why I chose to cut the pieces in that order. Each of these pieces has longer cuts than our practice pieces. But the technique remains the same. Keep the saw vertical and rotate the work piece smoothly. Balance your focus between the pencil line and the saw stroke.

Marquetry is a process of adding one piece of veneer after another to create an image. One of the methods of working very cleanly is to have each piece overlap into another piece that will be cut later. With a red pencil, I'll draw the area I'm going to cut out. Along the perimeter of the leaf, I'll follow the drawing. But in the interior of the leaf, I'll overlap into the other half of the leaf. The reason for this is we don't want to have to cut any line twice. So, in this example, piece #1 will overlap all the way into piece #3. Then, when piece #2 is cut, it will leave a very clean line between #1 and #2. When I cut the second piece, it will also overlap into piece #3. In this design, that will allow us to make #2 larger and easier to handle. Finally, #3 will clean up #2 and complete the design.

Now, decide the Douglas fir's orientation. I want the grain pattern of the fir to suggest the veins in the leaf, so I'll use the three short pencil lines in this leaf half as a guide.

With the grain orientation confirmed, tape the two pieces together.

Remember, I'm cutting around the piece in a clockwise direction. Therefore, I locate the drill hole in the easiest place to begin and end the cut—all the way over on the longer, relatively straighter line on piece #3. This is also the easiest place to hide the drill hole, because another piece of marquetry (piece #2) is going to cut this area out later.

Drill the hole here. I always exaggerate the tilt of the pin vise. Even though this part of the insert piece won't be seen in the end, I always practice the technique of over-angling the hole.

Thread the blade through the work piece as usual.

Slide the work piece along the blade to the handle. Flex the saw frame with your shoulder and tighten the clamp.

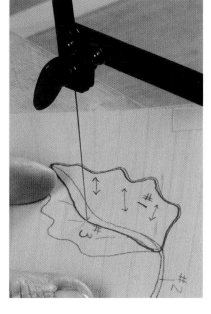 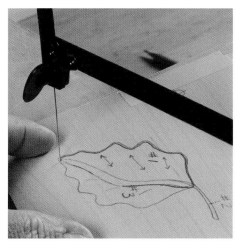 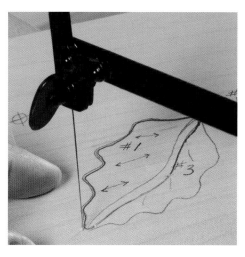

Position the work piece on the donkey, with the blade near the back of the bird's mouth. Check that the saw is vertical and begin cutting.

On this half of the leaf, the leaf point is a soft curve. I'm able to cut wide while the saw is in piece #3. Move slowly around the corner.

Rotate the work piece slowly as the blade tracks around the corner.

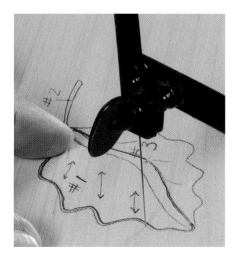 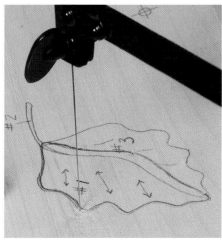 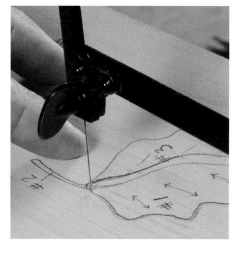

On the perimeter of the leaf, cut on the black pencil line, which is the actual edge of the pattern.

Sawing smoothly along the outline of the leaf.

At this point, cross over the stem and follow the red line around the corner.

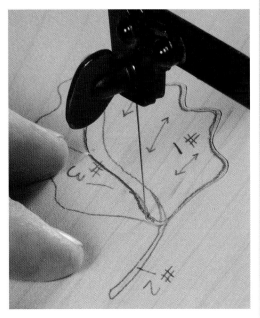

Headed back toward the end of the cut.

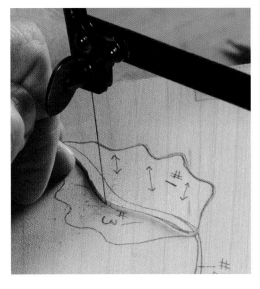

Aim toward the earlier saw kerf as you complete the cut. Move the work piece to the right side of the bird's mouth to keep the pieces from falling. Loosen the blade clamp and remove the saw.

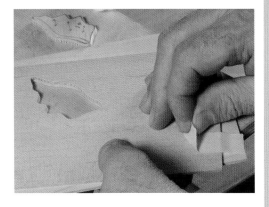

Set aside the waste pieces and remove the tape.

It's a nice, tight fit. I'll glue it in place.

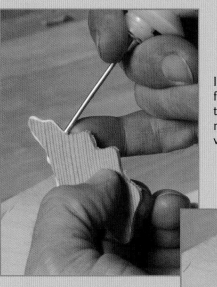

I like to keep my pinky finger touching the tip of the glue bottle. This helps me guide the glue line very easily and evenly.

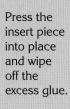

Press the insert piece into place and wipe off the excess glue.

Tap the piece until it is flush with the front side of the background veneer.

Insert piece #1 is glued in place. We are ready to begin work on the stem.

Preparing for the second piece. The first cut overlapped the other pieces of the design, so I'll need to replace the pencil line that I cut away. Reposition the vellum using the locator marks we drew on the pattern. Once aligned, tape the vellum in place. One piece of tape is enough.

Slide the graphite paper under the pattern, dark side down. Using the stylus, trace over the centerline, which was cut away. There's no need to retrace the whole pattern, just the center vein line.

Check to make sure the graphite transferred to the work piece. If there's no line, the graphite paper is probably upside down.

Piece #2 in the design is the stem, which will be made of English walnut. I want to position the English walnut so the grain direction runs parallel to the general direction of the stem.

I'll tape the background veneer and the insert veneer together and double-check that the stem pencil line on the background veneer lines up over the English walnut.

I also tape the pieces together on the underside.

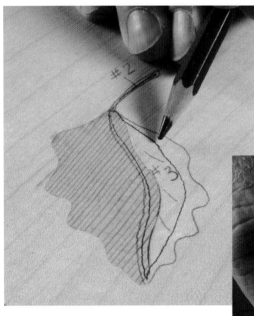

As before, when I cut piece #2, I will actually overlap into piece #3. The new red line shows where I'll be cutting. This method of always overlapping into another piece is a very freeing way of working. In this design, it will allow me to end up with a very thin line for the center vein. But the piece of wood I cut out for the center vein is actually a larger, easier size to work with, because piece #3 will cut away most of piece #2.

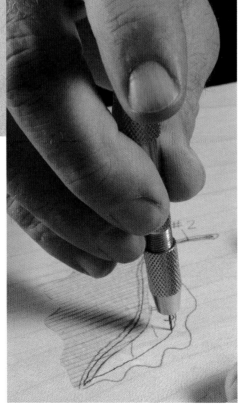

Again, my starting point for the drill location is in piece #3 (viewed here from the opposite side of the bench). As always, I'll be cutting in a clockwise direction. I always practice making the hole disappear in the insert piece. So my drill angle is steeper than vertical.

Here's the exit hole viewed from the underside.

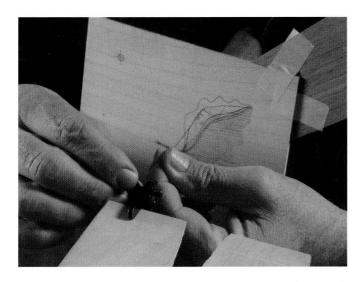

Hang the fret saw on the donkey, flex the blade into place, and tighten the clamp.

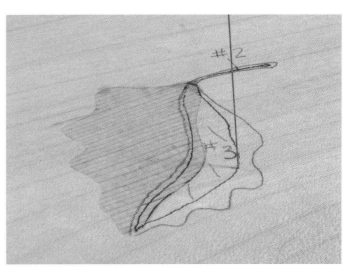

With the work piece in place, I'm ready to begin sawing. The saw is vertical and the blade is near the back of the bird's mouth.

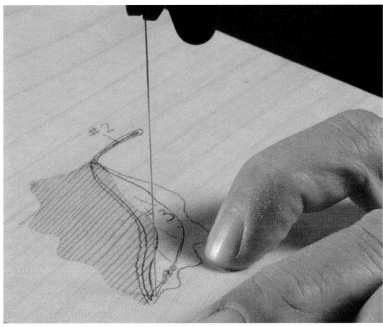

While I'm working in piece #3, the sawing is very casual. Once I reach the tip of the leaf and turn the corner, I'll focus on following the center vein pencil line very closely. Notice where the first two fingers of my left hand are. The bottom veneer is very narrow, so I want to be careful that I put pressure on the work piece over the walnut. Otherwise I might accidentally tip the work piece, which would change the sawing angle.

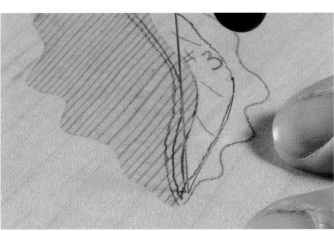

A close-up of the tip of the leaf: notice I'm sawing within the perimeter line of piece #3, but hugging that line pretty closely. This will give me a little more room to turn the corner and safely cut along the centerline.

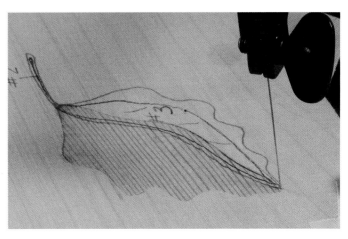

As I reach the corner, I slow down a little and stop pushing forward on the saw. I push the handle of the saw forward and as I begin rotating the work piece, I pull back slightly on the saw.

As I complete the corner, I check that my saw is vertical and begin cutting on the centerline.

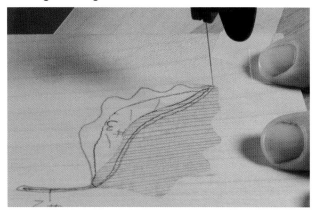

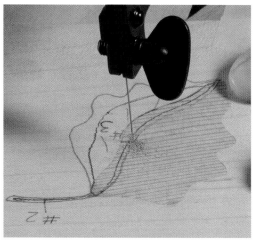

Sawing up the centerline, I follow the line as closely as I can, while being aware of the saw's vertical position. Every once in a while I stop sawing and move the saw and work piece side to side to be sure I'm still in the middle of the bird's mouth.

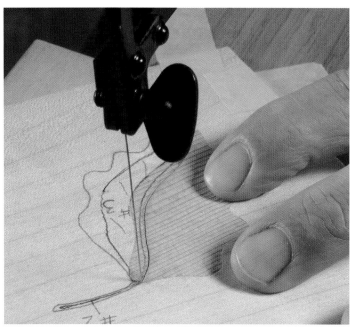

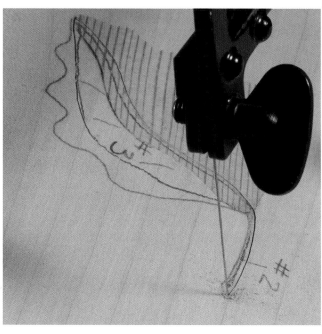

Now I exit the leaf and continue sawing along the stem. I want this curving line to be believable, so I may leave the pencil line for a short distance in order to create a nice curve. The transition between the leaf and the stem is important for making the image look natural.

I've reached the first corner of the stem. Again, stop forward pressure and push the handle a little forward under the donkey. As the work piece begins to rotate, pull back slightly on the saw.

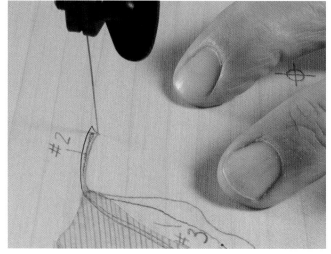

Saw along the short tip of the stem.

Carefully turn the last corner and saw a nice, curving line toward the leaf

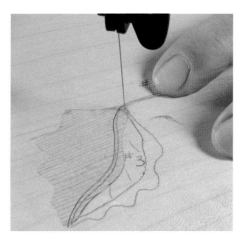

Once the blade enters the leaf in piece #3, I can turn away from the centerline and cut along the red line.

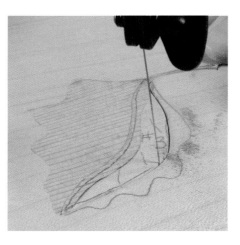

As I reach the starting point, I'm looking closely at the kerf from the beginning of the cut. In this case, this area of the design will be cut away by the last piece. But I want to always practice making a smooth transition near the drill hole.

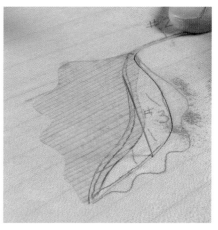

Release the top blade clamp and remove the saw.

Remove the tape and separate the pieces.

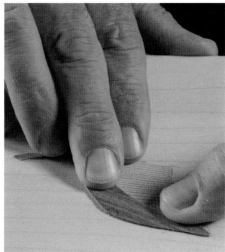

It looks like the fit will be nice.

Apply glue to the edge, press the piece into place, and tap with a hammer if necessary.

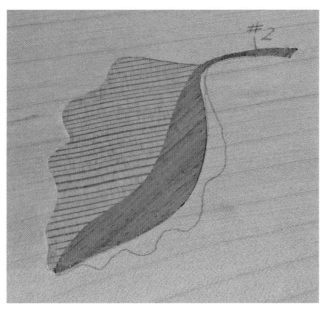

Piece #2 glued in place. Most of this piece will be replaced by piece #3.

Rather than use the pattern to redraw the second edge of the centerline, I'll draw it by hand. The center vein is very thin and I'll be able to draw this line a little easier by eye.

The new pencil line on piece #3 represents the grain direction for this side of the leaf. Remember, we cut out a piece from the Douglas fir for piece #1. For piece #3, be sure to position the fir so that the grain is going in the right direction and there are no holes in the veneer placed under the shape being cut.

With the grain direction oriented correctly, tape the veneers together.

On this last piece, the drill hole won't be cut away by a following piece. So, the pin vise needs to be tilted a little more. I need to decide where the hole will be located. I don't want to put it on the center vein because that line is going to be so thin. If I'm a little off the mark, either in drilling or sawing, the vein will have a jagged line. Instead, I'll put the drill along the perimeter of the leaf shape, away from the corners and in a place that is easy to begin and end sawing. This location puts me in a good position to have a successful cut.

Thread the blade through the work piece.

The saw is vertical and the blade is in the center of the bird's mouth.

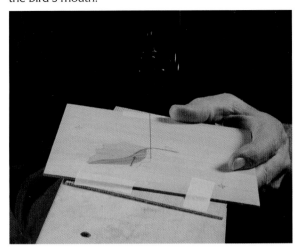

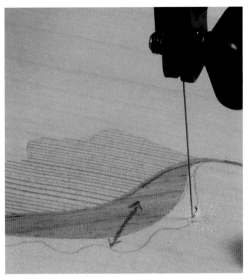

This pair of veneers is similar in size. If the bottom veneer were much smaller than the top, I would want to be careful not to tip the work piece with my left hand. I want to keep everything flat on the donkey so my sawing angle is accurate.

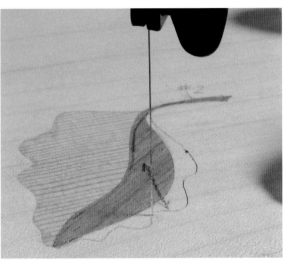

I am constantly checking the saw's angle and my location in the bird's mouth.

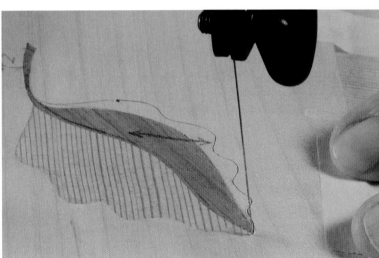

At the tip of the leaf, I'm aiming at the corner created by the other half of the leaf. I want both pieces of Douglas fir to touch at the same point at the leaf tip.

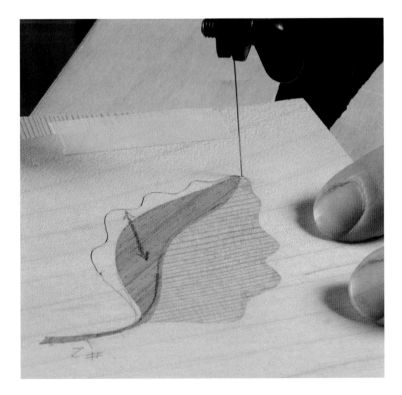

I make my corner when the saw blade touches the other piece of fir. For the first 1/2" or so, I actually want to be sawing the other piece of fir (piece #1). In other words, I don't want the English walnut center vein to go all the way to the tip. I want to suggest the finest of lines here, which is actually no line at all. The walnut vein will be a very fine point and will lead the eye to the tip of the leaf. In this case, I feel suggesting there is a vein here is better than actually leaving a thin line of walnut. In about 1/2" I'll ease the blade into the walnut. This will create a very fine point of walnut.

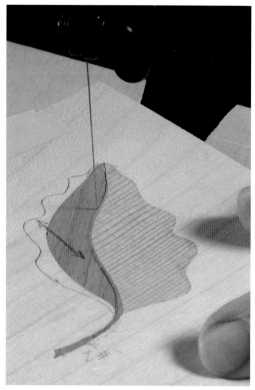

I've eased the blade over into the walnut now and I'm slowly leaving a fine dark line of walnut that will grow in width until I meet the stem.

I don't usually draw a pencil line when I want the insert color to be very fine—the saw blade is much thinner than a pencil line. Instead, I'm watching the sliver of walnut to my left of the saw blade. I'll slowly ease the width of the walnut vein to match the stem at the top of the leaf.

As I approach the starting point, I'm focused on the starting saw kerf. I want to blend right into that initial kerf. That will prevent a jagged shape where the hole was drilled.

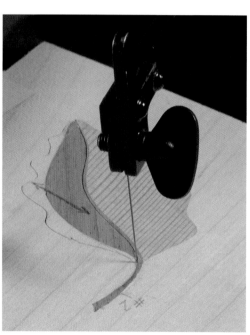

I've tried to aim the saw blade to this point, where the stem meets the leaf. I want this transition to be as natural as possible. When the saw blade meets the stem, I stop my forward pressure, begin rotating the work piece, and pull back slightly on the saw.

Complete the cut and release the top clamp.

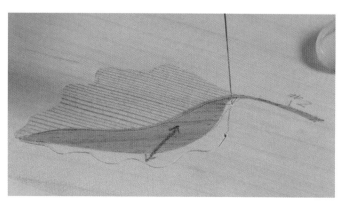

Having completed the turn, I'm back to the original pencil line.

Set the saw aside and lift the work piece.

Press the insert piece into the opening. The fit looks good.

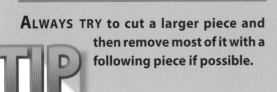

ALWAYS TRY to cut a larger piece and then remove most of it with a following piece if possible.

TIP

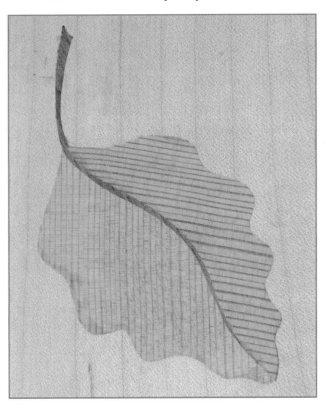

With the insert piece removed, notice the thin line of walnut left in the background piece. It's very fine and nicely balanced with the rest of the leaf. It would have been a little difficult to cut this long, narrow piece on it's own. However, by making the walnut piece a little larger initially and then cutting away most of it, the fine line was made very easily.

Apply glue to the insert piece.

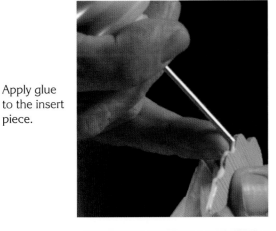

And tap it into place.

The finished marquetry piece features a simple design. The grain helps suggest the feeling of a leaf. Careful, enjoyable work helps create a nicely fitting, natural looking image.

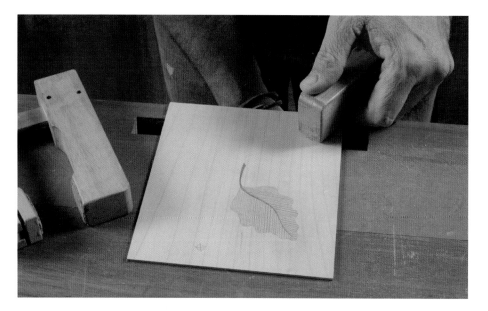

Now, scrape and sand the work piece flat. I need to work on both sides. The backside needs to be flat in preparation for gluing to a plywood core. I'll use a hand scraper or card scraper to get the veneer flat, then sandpaper to complete the flatness and make the surface smooth. I'm using wooden cam clamps to hold the veneer in place. Any light-duty clamps would work here.

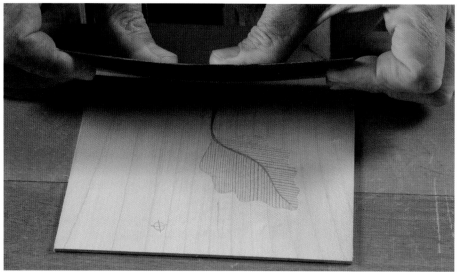

There are several ways to flatten and sand the veneer in preparation for gluing to a plywood core. With the veneer clamped, I'll begin to flatten the surface. A properly sharpened scraper is great for this job. Very quickly, I'll be able to flatten the veneer and uniformly level the surfaces.

The scraper can be pushed or pulled. I usually push, as I feel I can apply more control. The scraper is flexed slightly with the thumbs. Because it's flexed, only a short section of the blade is cutting at any time.

AS THE SCRAPER edge becomes dull, I'll scoot the scraper left or right in my grip to begin using a sharp area of the edge. A sharp scraper will make shavings. If it's making dust, it's time to freshen the edge. Here's the grip I am comfortable with. Notice the amount of pressure I'm applying to the scraper.

I want to keep the scraper fairly flat. If I flex it too much, I will make some low areas. A slightly flat scraper will take a little wider shaving and level the area very quickly.

I prefer to use the scraper for leveling the veneer because it's very fast and achieves a flat surface. The scraper also lets me skip using coarse sandpaper. When the surface is flat from the scraper, it's also very smooth and I only need to sand using finer grit paper.

TIP

The marquetry image is slightly below the background veneer. I'll begin scraping on the background to eventually level the complete surface. Move around the veneer to work the whole piece evenly. The goal is to flatten the entire surface. Resist the temptation to only work on the marquetry area. If I focus only on the marquetry, I'll create a low spot. Instead, think of taking the whole surface to one consistent level.

When scraping the marquetry, look at the grain direction of the insert pieces. I want to scrape in the same direction as a majority of the insert pieces. Most wood species can be scraped in any direction, but be careful of the scraper tearing an insert piece. If you notice this happening, just change the direction you're scraping.

I've flattened one half of the veneer. Rotate the veneer 180 degrees.

Do the same amount of work to the other half. If the scraper is not making shavings, slide to another part of the edge to find a sharp area.

The surface feels very flat.

Flip the veneer over and repeat the process to create a flat surface.

Once the veneer is flat on both sides, I'll sand it smooth. Here I'm using a piece of 3/4" MDF as a work surface. The MDF is held in place between the bench dogs. A thin piece of veneer is glued or tacked at one edge to serve as a cleat.

The cleat is a little thicker than my veneer. I have an extra veneer under the marquetry veneer to shim it up slightly above the cleat. The pressure of my sanding block will keep it in place.

This is the sanding block. It's a piece of maple with a flat sole. I've glued gasket cork to the flat sole (available at automotive supply shops). The sanding block is sized for a 1/4 sheet of sandpaper. It measures 5" x 2 5/8" x 1 1/8" thick. The sanding block creates a very smooth surface.

I use 220- and 320-grit sandpaper for smoothing the surface. If I hadn't used the scraper, I would need to use much coarser sandpaper to do the leveling. But the scraper has already taken care of that. I only need to use these finer grits to finish the work.

The sandpaper wraps around the sanding block with the cork surface contacting the back of the paper.

I'll begin with the front side of the veneer. One hand holds the veneer against the cleat and the other hand grips the sandpaper tight against the block. I take full strokes, being careful not to round the edges and corners. Work carefully to keep the sanding block flat on the surface for the length of the stroke.

When one side is sanded smooth with the 220, change to the 320-grit paper and carefully sand the surface again. Once smooth, turn the piece to sand the bottom side of the veneers. This is the glue side, so it doesn't need to be as fine. I prefer to leave this surface at 220 grit so the glue surface has a little more bite.

The sanded veneer is ready to be glued to a piece of plywood. I've also sanded a piece of veneer for the back of the plywood, called a backer veneer. This veneer balances the plywood panel, preventing it from warping and should always be used.

The plywood acts as a core, which will be sandwiched between the two veneers. The plywood can be any thickness, depending on the type of project being made. I'm using a piece of cherry for the backer veneer on this panel.

This is the 1/8" Baltic birch plywood I'll use for the core of the panel. Before I cut it to size, I'll draw some pencil lines on one side. This will help me assemble the two veneer pieces for the core with their faces opposing each other. I'm ready to make the panel. It will be made up of two veneers and two pieces of thin plywood.

Plywood Core

Here are my thoughts on the plywood core. For this project I've decided I want a 1/4" core. This will be a nice finished dimension for a jewelry box lid, wall hanging, or any other project that requires a thin panel. I could use 1/4" plywood for the core. But I prefer to build up the core from thinner plywood. In my experience, this leads to a flatter core.

Plywood is rarely perfectly flat when purchased. The veneer we are gluing to the plywood won't have an effect on the flatness of the core. If the core is a little warped, the veneer is not going to help straighten it.

To help assure I have the flattest core possible, I glue up thinner plywood to arrive at the thickness I need. For this project, I want a 1/4" core; so, combining two pieces of 1/8" plywood will give me the 1/4" thickness. The 1/8" plywood is also not flat, but if I arrange the two pieces so any curve or warping opposes each other, I'll have a very flat panel.

I use this process for the cores in my veneered furniture work. For example, if I need a 1" thick core for a tabletop, I'll glue up four layers of 1/4" plywood—alternating any curves or twists. This has worked very well for me and I rarely have a situation where the core for a project is anything other than flat.

There are other materials that can be used as the core, in particular MDF. It's very flat and readily available. However, I prefer to use good plywood such as Baltic birch plywood, available from many woodworking stores. I purchase 1/4" and 1/8" pieces and then create any thickness I need.

I'll arrange the veneers and plywood so that the grain direction of the veneers opposes the grain direction of the plywood. This is a common practice in all veneer work and will help balance the panel a little, minimizing any chance of warping.

I cut the plywood and veneers to the same dimension using the table saw, keeping the grain orientation in mind as I work. The veneers and plywood on my project measure 6 1/2" x 5 3/4".

I'm using a sliding table, table saw to cut the 1/8" plywood to size. With a long, straight edge of the plywood against the saw's crosscut fence, I square one end.

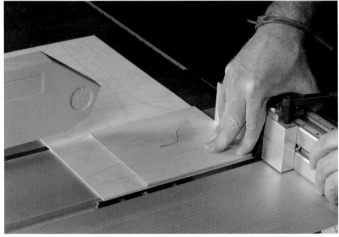

I flip the plywood end for end, so I can reference off the new, square cut. I want to cut the plywood and veneers together so they're all the same size. I've got the grain of the plywood and veneer opposing each other. My hands are safely away from the path of the blade.

I rotate the package, cutting until I've squared all four edges.

The finished set (*left to right*): marquetry veneer, cherry backer veneer, and two pieces of 1/8" plywood.

Pencil lines indicating the grain direction of each piece.

This is the last step prior to the glue-up phase. After stacking the set in order (marquetry veneer, plywood, plywood, and backer veneer), draw a cabinetmaker's triangle on one edge. This will help realign the set if they become shuffled out of place during the glue-up.

This is a simple way to glue up a small work piece, using supplies already in the shop. The method consists of four pieces of 3/4" MDF, kraft paper or newspaper, regular f-style woodworking clamps, a glue spreader, blue tape, and yellow or white woodworking glue. I use a plastic glue spreader available from any hardware store. The smallest set of teeth leave a nice amount of glue. The four pieces of MDF will serve as the caul for the glue-up, distributing flat, even pressure from the clamps. The paper helps prevent the work piece from becoming glued to the MDF cauls.

Tear off about four pieces of blue tape and fold one end on itself. This makes a tab you can use for easily pulling the tape off after the glue-up. Stick the tape to the good side of the marquetry veneer. Good organization is important for a successful, calm glue-up. Have everything ready before applying glue.

Place the marquetry veneer on the bench with the good side down. Apply glue to the first piece of plywood and flip the plywood onto the marquetry veneer. I want to apply glue to the plywood rather than the veneer, because the veneer will begin to warp once the glue is on its surface. This is less of a problem with these thick sawn veneers, but it's a good habit to get into.

Apply glue to the second piece of plywood, spread evenly with the spreader, and flip on to the first piece of plywood.

Finally, apply glue to the backside of the second piece of plywood and spread evenly.

Flip the backer veneer on top of the plywood, line all the pieces up together, and pull the tape tight across the package.

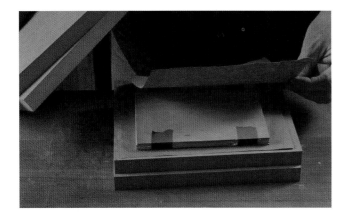

I put two pieces of MDF on the bench, a piece of paper on top of those, and then the work piece. Then I place paper on top of the work piece. The remaining two pieces of MDF finish the glue-up assembly.

Four clamps are enough for this small glue-up. Position the clamps so they are over the work piece and applying pressure evenly. There should be small drops of glue squeezing out around the edges of the work piece. Let the glue dry for an hour or two.

With the glue dry, remove the clamps and cauls. The tape is easy to remove because of the tabs we folded before the glue-up. Sometimes the tape can tear the grain of the wood a little. This is more prevalent with some species. To help minimize the chance of tearing fibers, pull the tape off at an angle to the edge of the work piece.

The tape kept the pieces from sliding around too much during the glue-up, but they shifted a little. The edges can be cleaned up with a small plane. If the piece were longer, I would feel comfortable jointing the edge on the jointer. The other three edges can then be cut to size on the table saw.

First I'll cut away some of the dried glue with a knife.

A few strokes with a short plane straighten the edge and square it to the face.

Check with a square to be sure the edge is 90° to the face.

The finished edge.

Square both ends of the work piece on the table saw. Here is the first cut.

Flip end for end and cut the second end. Keep the straight edge against the fence for both cuts.

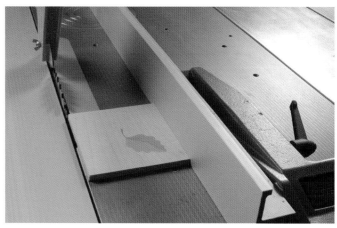

Then rip the last edge parallel to the jointed edge. Here's the set up. Be sure to lock the rip-fence down and use a riving knife and safety guards.

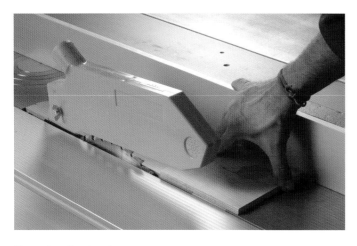

Preparing for the rip cut.

Back at the bench: the squared panel.

The last step for this project will be applying edge banding to the edges of the piece. This will frame the marquetry as well as hide the plywood. I'll use narrow pieces of sawn walnut veneer with straight grain for this edge banding. The finished panel is 3/8" thick. I'll use a knife and straightedge to cut the walnut veneer into strips that are about 1/2" wide.

The walnut strips ready to glue to the edges.

The strips can be cut about 1/2" longer than the work piece. I've torn off pieces of blue tape (about 4" long), which will be used to "clamp" the edge banding to the panel.

Apply glue to the edge of the panel.

Spread the glue evenly and position the edge banding in place. It needs to overhang both faces of the panel as well as the ends.

Tightly stretch a piece of tape over each end of the edge banding. I feel with my fingertips to be sure the edge banding is overhanging both faces.

Cover the rest of the edge banding with tightly stretched blue tape.

Repeat the process for the edge banding on the opposite side. This is a very successful way of applying a thin edging to a panel, especially smaller projects like this. Let the panel dry for about 30 minutes.

After the glue is dry, remove the tape and make the edge banding flush with the faces of the panel. I'm using a small hand plane to trim the walnut nearly flush.

Then, use a woodworking file to make the edge banding perfectly flush. I'm using an Oberg file made by Sandvik. I applied a couple layers of blue tape around the end of the file to protect the surface of the veneer. This helps me get a perfectly smooth finish. A sanding block could also be used. Be careful to keep the edge of the walnut crisp. Sanding tends to round edges slightly.

I apply pressure over the blue-taped tip of the file, while carefully pushing the file forward. In a few strokes I'll have a perfectly flat edge band.

After planing and filing the edges of both edge bandings, it's time to cut the ends of the walnut flush with the panel. There needs to be a perfect fit of walnut to walnut in the corner.

First, put two pieces of blue tape on the edge of the panel. These will act as a shim. I want to sneak up on a perfect fit. The tape allows me to cut very close to flush.

I'll use a flush-cut Japanese saw to trim the edge banding. The teeth of this saw have no set, so it does not damage the surface it is resting on.

Lay the saw on the blue tape shims. Apply pressure downwards and lightly saw the walnut edge banding.

Using the same taped woodworking file, take a few gentle strokes to make the edge banding perfectly flush with the panel. I'm applying pressure on the tip of the file, keeping it very flat on the edge of the panel. Files only cut on the push stroke. Lift the file to return to the starting position after each stroke. This will protect the fibers at the corner of the edge banding.

Remove the tape and set it aside. I'll use the same tape shim for all four corners.

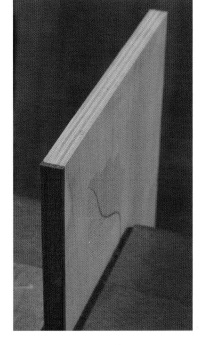

With one corner finished, reuse the tape shim and trim and file the remaining corners.

Careful work has left perfectly sharp, clean corners.

Cut the two remaining edge band pieces a little longer than the work piece. Prepare six or eight short pieces of tape. Apply glue to the edge of the panel.

Spread the glue evenly across the edge.

Position the edge banding in place. Use the fingertips to be sure the walnut overhangs the faces and ends of the panel.

Stretch a piece of tape tightly over both ends of the edge banding. Then finish taping the length of the panel.

The tape is pressing tightly against the edge banding, causing some glue to squeeze-out. This is an indication of the proper amount of glue.

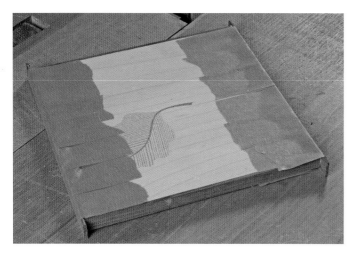

Complete the opposite edge and set aside for 30 minutes.

Remove the tape and the edge banding is nearly complete.

Again, use a small plane to cut the walnut nearly flush with the veneer surface. I'm planing slightly toward the panel. This allows me to keep one corner of the plane in contact with the panel surface, helping prevent an accidental outward bevel on the edge banding. Protect the adjacent walnut edges from the bench dogs with heavy cardboard or mat board.

Careful work with the file brings the walnut flush with the panel. The pressure is applied to the nose of the file.

Place two pieces of tape on the previously completed walnut edge to create a shim.

Applying pressure directly over the tape, carefully cut the overhanging walnut. Repeat on all four corners.

Use the file to trim the walnut perfectly flush with the adjacent edge. Again, a good woodworking file will leave much better results than sand paper for this step, because the file will keep the edges square and crisp rather than rounding over. Remember only cut on the push stroke, lifting the file each time when pulling back.

Holding the panel in the tail vise, sand both sides of the panel smooth and flat. I'm using a cork-faced sanding block with 220-grit sand paper. I work carefully when sanding near the edges, so that I don't round over the corners. Use straight strokes, sanding with the grain of the veneer.

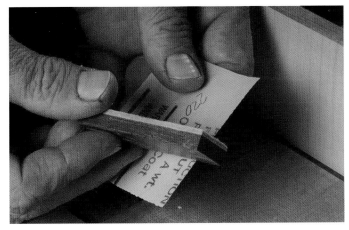

The edges can be hand planed or sanded. For sanding the edges, wrap 220-grit sand paper around a small, wooden sanding block. I've applied a thick piece of artist mat board to pad this sanding block.

Sand the walnut edges flat and smooth.

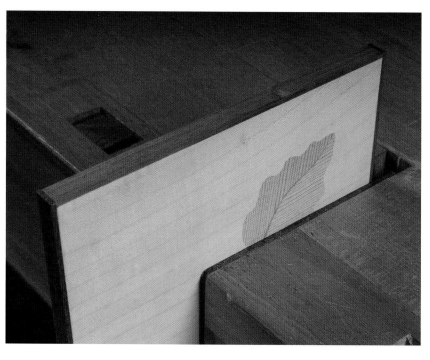

Once the edges are sanded flat, use the sanding block to soften the corners, making them friendlier to touch.

Clean, careful work has produced a nice fitting edge band that hides the plywood core and frames the marquetry image.

The completed panel is ready for a finish.

Shellac

The finish I prefer to use for projects like cabinets and boxes is shellac. Shellac is very easy to prepare, apply, and repair, if necessary. The wood surface takes on a rich, subtle sheen that feels good to the touch and doesn't hide the grain of the wood.

For this project, I'll use super blonde shellac flakes dissolved in a small amount of denatured alcohol. There are other grades of shellac flakes such as orange and garnet. I'm using super blonde because it has the lightest tone and only a small amount of natural wax.

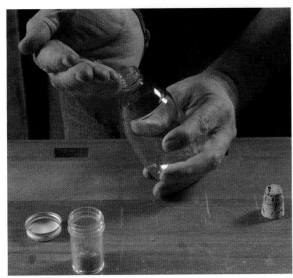

To mix shellac, pour a small amount of flakes into a clear glass bottle, filling it about 1/2" deep.

Then, use a funnel to pour denatured alcohol into the bottle, filling to about 1/2" above the flakes.

This looks about right. The ratio isn't really important. This mixture will become my thick base. After the flakes have dissolved, I'll pour a small amount into another bottle and dilute much more to make the working shellac.

Cork or cap the bottle and let the flakes dissolve overnight. I usually give the bottle a shake now and then to stir up the dissolving flakes.

Once dissolved, the base shellac should be very thick and look like this. This small, concentrated amount of thick shellac will make many bottles of diluted shellac.

I lightly shake the bottle and put a little on my finger to test the mixture. The color of the working shellac is much more yellow and clear than the thick base shellac.

THE AMOUNT of shellac to alcohol is not really that important, which means the protection or beauty the finish provides is not affected if it's a little too thick or a little too thin. If the mixture is a little thin, it just means it might take longer to build up sheen. And if it's too thick, it builds up too quickly and becomes a little tacky and difficult to create an even sheen.

TIP

I pour a very small amount of thick shellac into a second clear glass bottle to about 1/2" deep. This is the bottle I'll work from when applying shellac to the work piece.

Then I fill the bottle most of the way to the top with denatured alcohol. I don't fill the new bottle all the way to the top in case I have to adjust the mixture.

Initially my finger and thumb will stick as I rub them together, then after a few seconds, as the alcohol evaporates, the shellac should gloss over and rub easily. This is just right. If my fingers stay very sticky and never gloss over, I've got too much shellac in the bottle and I need to dilute it with a little more alcohol. If my fingers never get sticky, the mixture was too diluted to begin with and I need to add a little more thick shellac. It's very unscientific in a satisfying way and very effective.

A properly mixed working shellac mixture (*left*) and the thick, base shellac (*right*). Be sure the bottles are capped to reduce evaporation.

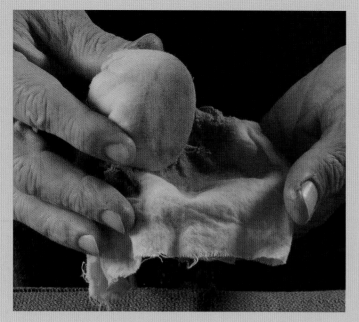

I apply shellac with a fad, which is a cloth folded into a tight ball. Linen or cotton work well. I usually make the fad from two pieces of cloth. The first piece is folded until it becomes a thick square, which when squeezed is shaped a little bit like a ball. The second piece of cloth wraps around the ball.

This second cloth is in contact with the surface of the wood. Over time, it becomes torn with use and needs to be shifted and moved around to create a new, smooth surface on the bottom of the ball. Without the second piece of cloth, I would need to replace the ball itself often, as it would be the one damaged by use. By using the same ball for years sometimes, it becomes saturated with shellac, which builds up a nice finish more quickly.

Holding the fad tight and round, I apply shellac in straight, overlapping strokes in the same direction as the grain of the background veneer.

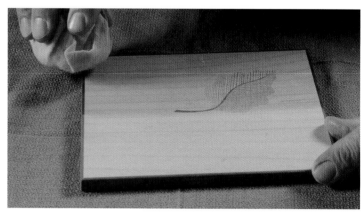

Lift the stroke off the end of the work piece evenly. I don't want to let the fad stop on the work piece, so I keep it moving off the edge.

After 10 or 12 passes I let the surface dry for a few minutes. The alcohol evaporates very quickly and the shellac begins drying almost immediately. While the shellac is drying, I begin the same process on the edges of the panel.

All four edges and the marquetry surface have one coat of shellac. I can already see the finish beginning to build. I'll repeat a few more times until I begin to get the finish surface I'm looking for. Then I'll let this dry for about 20 minutes, until it no longer feels damp.

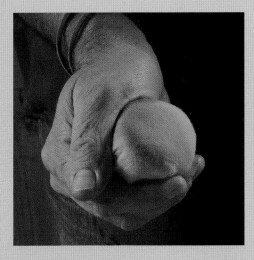

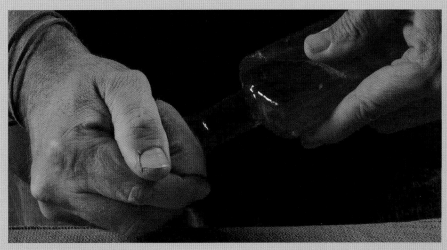

I wrap the cloth around the ball very tightly, keeping the bottom of the fad wrinkle-free and dome shaped. This helps apply the shellac evenly.

Add some shellac to the fad. When using a new fad, I usually need to add shellac quite often. Once the fad becomes saturated over time, I don't need to add too much. I don't want the fad to be too wet.

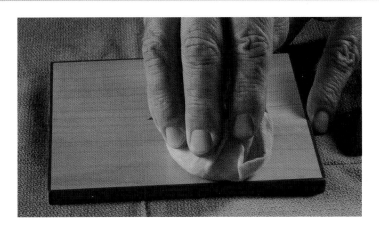

Working my way across the surface.

I repeat this process of working across the surface 10 or 12 times without waiting for the shellac to dry. The shellac will slowly begin building up with each pass.

After 15 or 20 minutes, I'll work on the back of the panel just as I did the front.

Once the back has dried a little while, I return to the front side. I add a little more shellac to the fad, but only enough to dampen it. As I get closer to completing the finish, I'll gradually apply less shellac. At the end, the fad will be pretty dry.

After another coat on the marquetry surface, I'll apply another coat to the edges. I'm counting 10 or 12 passes across the surface as one coat.

After the second coat has had some time to dry—maybe 45 minutes—I'll carefully rub the surface with #0000 steel wool (pronounced four aught). The steel wool evens out the shellac and smoothes any roughness on the wood. I usually do this after each coat, although I sometimes apply a second coat before rubbing it out the first time, just to have a nice amount of shellac on the surface before I use the steel wool.

If I feel any unevenness on the wood surface, I sometimes lightly sand the first coat of shellac with worn out 400-grit sand paper. I wear it out by rubbing it against itself. After this first sanding, I use #0000 steel wool for all the following coats.

Rubbing with firm and even pressure with the grain.

Rubbing out the edges. I repeat all the shellac steps until I get the finish I want—usually a subtle sheen. With a wood species like maple, I usually arrive at the look I'm after in about 5 or 6 coats (one coat equals 10 or 12 passes across the surface). Other wood species may take more or less coats to build up a nice finish. I always use the steel wool between coats to help even out the finish.

After the last shellac coat has been rubbed out, I dust the surface and the work area to remove the small fragments of steel wool. At this stage the wood surface has a nice, even sheen and is ready for wax. Wax will give the panel a small amount of protection against fingerprints and adds a little extra shine to the piece. Here I'm applying soft beeswax with a small piece of cloth. I let the wax dry for 5 or 10 minutes and then rub it out with #0000 steel wool. Dust the panel again and the project is finished.

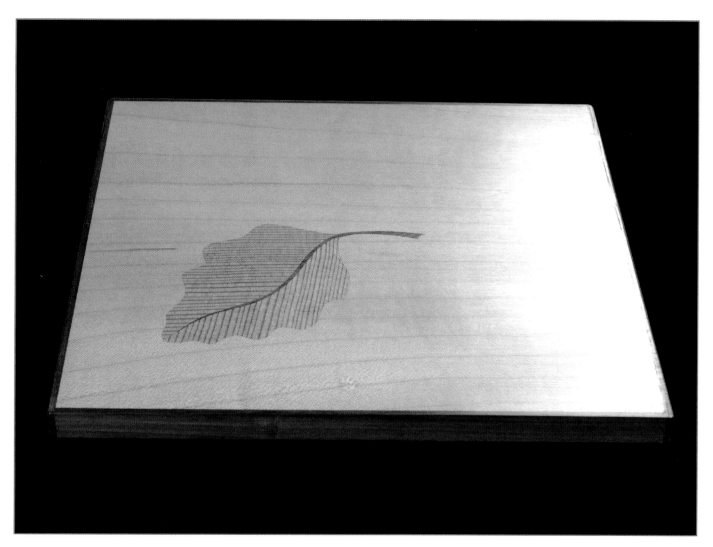

The completed marquetry panel.

Lotus Marquetry Box

Creating a Mockup

When designing a new piece, whether it's a cabinet, table, or small box, I begin with a simple, full size mockup. The mockup helps me get the balance of the proportions right and feel comfortable about the design before I begin making the piece.

The mockup can be made of any inexpensive material. For a cabinet or table mockup, I usually use a combination of thin plywood, cardboard, and construction 2 x 4s, which I mill to the dimensions I need. The mockup is assembled with double-sided tape, drywall screws, or hot glue—any material that can be worked with easily. My goal with the mockup is to be able to assemble it and modify it very easily. After all, I'm only trying to achieve pleasing proportions at this stage. The details and subtle elements of the design can come later. The mockup is a three-dimensional sketch and a good starting point for the project. It gives me confidence to move forward with lumber selection and construction of the piece.

The project for this section is a small box with a marquetry design on the top. Thick cardboard or mat-board (about 1/8" thick, available at art supply stores) works well for this small mockup.

I have a general idea about the approximate size of the box I'd like to make. As a beginning point, I'm imagining a box about 4" x 6" and a couple of inches tall. If I'm unsure about the dimensions of the box, I usually make the mockup a little larger initially, and then trim down the size later if it seems too big.

I try to make mockups as simple as possible. For the box project, I cut 2 long strips using a knife and straight edge. The strips measure 2 1/4" wide and more than 12" long.

Then, cut both strips to 10 1/4" long. This 2 1/4" x 10 1/4" strip of cardboard represents one side and one end of the box mockup (6" + 4 1/4" = 10 1/4").

On each strip, make a mark at 6" and using the straight edge, score the cardboard. This allows the cardboard strips to be bent—each bend creates a corner of the box.

I score and bend the cardboard just to make taping the mockup together a little easier. In other words, by scoring the long strips and bending the cardboard, I only have to tape two corners together. Here the strips are butted together and taped.

The remaining corner is taped in place.

A rectangular piece of cardboard on top completes the mockup. Now I have a three-dimensional object that can help me decide on the proportions of the jewelry box, cabinet, table, etc. The mockup only took a few minutes to make and is easily changed if I feel the proportions are out of balance. It's invaluable for helping me feel comfortable with the size of a project.

I've chosen a piece of narra for the box. Narra is a very fragrant hardwood from Papua New Guinea. The wood is easy to work with and has a nice luster when finished. It will also be a nice background color and texture for the marquetry design I'm planning.

The mockup has helped me arrive at the dimensions for the box, which allows me to layout the piece of narra. I've used chalk to layout the section of the board that will become the top panel (right). I prefer to use straighter grain for the box sides. The narrow, marked section on the near side of the board has fairly straight grain, so I'll use this for the four sides of the box. The other narrow section on the far side of the board has grain running at an angle. Later, when I rip this part of the board, I'll set this piece aside as an extra.

Use a band saw or table saw to cut off the piece that will become the top panel veneers. Before beginning to saw the piece into veneers, draw a cabinetmaker's triangle on one end.

Determine the drift of the band saw blade again if necessary. Set the fence about 3/32" from the blade and with a slow, steady feed rate, begin re-sawing the first veneer.

Once I begin cutting, I move steadily through the cut, being careful not to pause, which will often leave a bump in the veneer. I use a push stick as I approach the end. I'll cut the remaining veneers one after another, without re-jointing the short board. If the board is long enough to joint safely, a light pass over the jointer will clean up any unevenness left by the band saw cut.

It's important that my veneers are 5/64" thick. Since I'm not jointing after each veneer is cut, I'm sawing to the final thickness of 5/64". This is possible because the band saw is carefully tuned and cutting well, so I get a very smooth surface from the saw. I could also saw the veneers a little thicker and use a drum sander to arrive at 5/64".

The finished veneers: two veneers will be used for the box lid and the extra two can be used for marquetry on future projects.

The sketch on top is my original drawing of a lotus petal for the marquetry project. The sketch below is a tracing from the original drawing on vellum paper. The tracing will be used for the marquetry pattern. See pattern in back of book.

The lotus petal is white, so I've chosen some light colored woods for the marquetry: maple, birch, and holly (*left to right*).

I cut the tracing paper down a little so it's more in scale with the marquetry project. After deciding where I want the marquetry image to be positioned on the veneer, I tape it in position with a single piece of tape.

Using a stylus and graphite paper, transfer the pattern onto the veneer

The transferred image.

I'll leave the pattern taped to the veneer until I finish the marquetry. This will allow me to easily retrace the lines of the pattern after they are cut away.

Sand Shading

In addition to the normal marquetry tools, I'll use a hot plate and small pan to heat sand. The hot sand is used to shade individual pieces of marquetry to help create a sense of depth and give the marquetry image the illusion of being three-dimensional. I find that fine grain sand, available at pet stores, works very well for marquetry.

I try to use sand shading very carefully, as it's easy to over-shade the wood—making the marquetry pieces look burned or charred. I prefer to use a light touch with shading, allowing the viewer's eye to "see" a three-dimensional image.

Another way to say that is, I don't want to think "sand shading", when I see the completed marquetry image. With that in mind, when I use the sand shading technique, I try to be consistent with the amount of shading on individual pieces. I'm careful to choose wood species that shade nicely. Some woods develop a beautiful tone when shaded with hot sand. Maple falls into that category. It's very nice when shaded—the darker tone is very subtle.

Other species, to my eye, are not as effective when shaded. For example, poplar sometimes has a green color, but when shaded it does not become a deeper green. Instead, it appears charred and a little unnatural.

To practice sand shading, use the fret saw to cut a small piece from a light colored veneer.

I've turned on the hot plate to the high setting and put a small amount of sand in an inexpensive pan. After the sand is hot, I hold the small piece of wood with a long hemostat or tweezers and dip one edge into the hot sand for about 20 seconds.

The shading has a nice, graduated amount of color. If a darker tone is needed, another 15 or 20 seconds in the hot sand will probably be enough. The amount of time needed to shade the piece depends mostly on the temperature of the hot plate. I want the shading to happen quickly because the longer the wood is in contact with the hot sand, the more likely it is to shrink a little. This is particularly prevalent across the grain, which means the piece will no longer fit tightly in the marquetry panel.

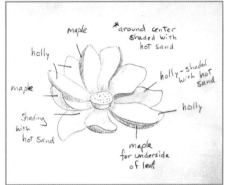

Back to the original sketch: I've added some pencil shading to the lotus design to help visualize where the individual pieces will be shaded. I've also identified where I want to use the maple and holly. I'll keep this "map" nearby for reference as I work.

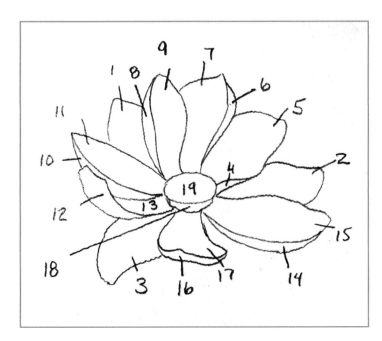

On a separate tracing, I've identified the sequence in which I'll work. I'll always start working on the parts of the image that appear farther away and gradually move to the parts that appear closer. For example, petal #1 (upper left) appears behind petal #11 and petals #8 and #9. Petal #1 will be cut into place earlier in the process so that those petals appearing closer to my eyes have the illusion of being 'in front' of petal #1. See the numbered pattern in the back of the book.

Sometimes it's not clear if one piece is visually behind another piece. In that case I'll try to cut the simpler of the two pieces first. I'm trying not to paint myself into a corner by making sequence choices that create some very difficult cuts later. Notice the center of the lotus flower is left until the very end. This is so that each of the petals can ease into the center area and the flower center can cleanly trim all the petals at one time.

I've laid a new piece of vellum over the sequence drawing to show how each petal will overlap with its neighboring petals. I can drill the hole for the blade anywhere along the red dotted line and a following piece will cut the drill hole away.

Each of the individual petals will be shaded with hot sand. It's helpful to keep the red dotted line very close to the actual pencil line to ensure the sand shading can happen very quickly. For example, if the pieces overlap into the neighboring petals too much, the piece will need to be left in the hot sand a long time in order to shade the area that will actually be seen. Since the heat from the sand can shrink the marquetry piece, it's best to overlap only a small amount—1/16" works well.

The red dotted lines drawn on the background veneer.

I've drawn an arrow on petal #1 indicating the grain direction of the insert piece, which in this case is holly.

Taping the holly veneer in place.

Drilling for piece #1. Notice I've got the drill bit pretty close to the pencil line so I don't have to shade too much.

Threading the blade through the veneers. Notice the pattern is still taped in place on the background veneer.

Beginning the cut.

Approaching the tip of the petal. Here I'll push my sawing hand forward to help create a sharp point.

I've removed the blade to demonstrate the path I'm following with the saw blade. I cut on the red dotted line until the blade reached the top part of the petal at which point I began sawing on the actual black line. I'll continue sawing until I cut into the other neighboring petal, and then follow the red dotted line back to the drill hole.

The completed cut.

With the waste piece removed, it's easy to see the plan of attack for each petal in the lotus design. Every piece spills into its neighbor until the last piece.

The tight fitting holly petal is ready for shading.

I want to shade along this long edge, then the opposing edge.

The holly piece is slightly buried in the hot sand.

After 20-25 seconds, the holly receives nice, subtle shading.

The opposite long edge of the holly has a concave curve. To prevent burning the narrow ends of the holly, I reshape the sand into a small hill so the corners of the holly are not buried in the sand.

Shading the center of the concave curve while protecting the corners from charring.

The shaded petal. When judging whether I've shaded enough, it's important to remember that the darkest part of the shading will eventually be cut off when the neighboring pieces are made.

The petal, when glued into place, shows a nice fit at the top of the petal, but a little shrinking near the center of the flower. I don't feel I had the holly in contact with the hot sand for an unusually long time, so this is an indication that this holly may have a tendency to shrink in the heat.

My solution for this is to slightly increase my sawing angle, which will create a slightly tighter fitting piece. Each of the pieces in this design will be shaded, with the exception of the flower center. So, if I consistently make the pieces a fraction tighter than usual, I'll have a perfect fit after sand shading.

I can increase my sawing angle by shimming the donkey a little or by consciously sawing at a greater than vertical angle. The latter method is the one I will choose for this project. It's easy to feel like I'm tweaking the fit by sawing too steeply. Simply move the handle of the saw slightly to the left. A little extra goes a long way and it's easy to be consistent.

However, if you're just getting a feel for sawing by hand, you might prefer to shim the donkey with a scrap of veneer. Loosen the clamp, slide a veneer scrap under the right side of the donkey's base, and re-clamp.

Piece #2 is also holly. The pencil line shows the grain direction.

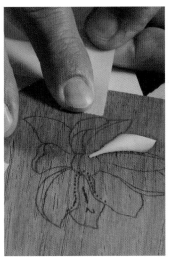

Taping the veneers together.

Drill the hole in the neighboring petal, near the pencil line.

I've drawn a circle around the exit hole to make it a little more visible.

Threading the saw blade.

Beginning the cut alongside the petal line.

At the corner I move the saw handle forward to help make a sharp corner.

Once the top of the petal is cut, I overlap the cut into the adjoining petal.

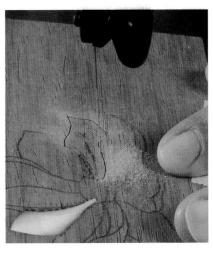

I cut slightly into the center of the flower before returning to the drill hole.

The completed cut.

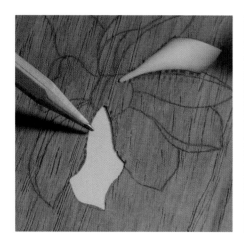

The fit of the holly insert piece is slightly tighter than usual. The two long edges need shading.

Checking the shaded sketch, I see that this piece of holly needs to be shaded all the way towards the center of the flower.

Again, I am shading in a small hill of sand to prevent the narrow corner from being over shaded.

The first edge, with shading.

Both long edges shaded. Holding the insert piece near the design helps determine if the amount of shading is similar to the first petal.

Glue the edges of the insert piece.

Press the insert piece in place...

And tap it flush.

The first two pieces are finished. The shading is subtle and consistent. The fit of the second piece is nice and tight after the sand shading. The small angle adjustment worked well.

Piece #3 is very similar to the previous petals.

The grain direction is marked in pencil and the holly taped in place. The holly veneer is becoming riddled with holes from cutting out the previous insert pieces, be sure there is wood below the petal before cutting!

Drill the hole near the pencil line.

Just like the previous two petals, I cut along the line then turn and cut the top of the petal.

Turning the sharp corner.

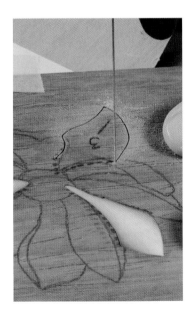

Overlap the cut into the adjacent petal.

Then, overlap into the center of the flower and finish the cut.

The fit is nice and slightly tight.

93

Again, the small hill of sand allows me a little more control over which areas get shaded and those narrow areas that need to be protected from overshading.

The amount of shading is consistent with the other pieces, so it can be glued in place.

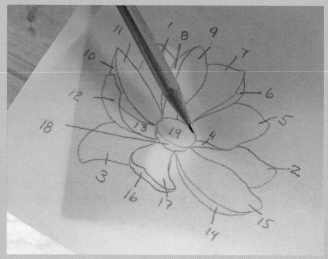

With these three completed, I can begin working on the petals that appear in the foreground.

Petal #4 is a small piece that represents the underside of petal #5.

The hard maple veneer will be just a little darker than the white holly.

The earlier holly piece cut away part of the pencil line for piece #4.

Retransfer missing lines with the stylus and graphite paper.

The new line.

Drill in the overlapping area, near the pencil line.

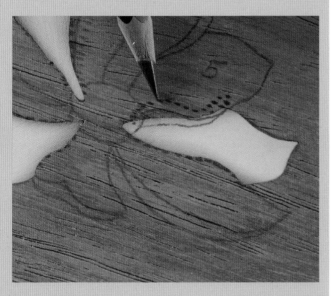

The red dotted line shows where I will overlap into the adjacent piece.

As I begin sawing, notice the slight adjustment to the sawing angle. I've increased the angle slightly by moving my sawing hand a little to my left. This will create a slightly tighter fit to compensate for the wood shrinking in the hot sand.

The maple is taped in place. Like the holly pieces, I'll position the grain of the small piece being cut lengthwise.

Beginning the cut.

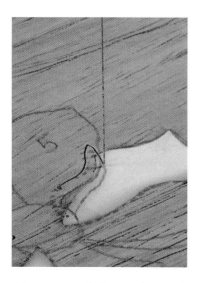

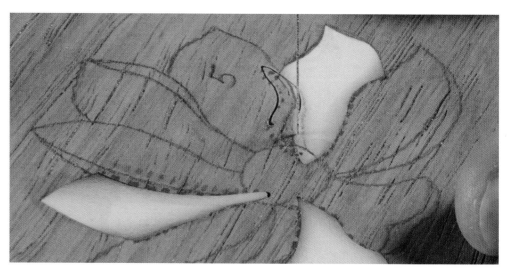

After sawing a little past the tip of the maple piece, I turn and saw along the line, into the holly.

I often improvise off of the pattern line to preserve some of the shaded tones. In other words, sometimes the shading does not extend past my pattern line, so cutting on the line would remove all the shading. Usually the design is not impacted by modifying the shape of an individual piece slightly on the fly, especially with subjects like flowers.

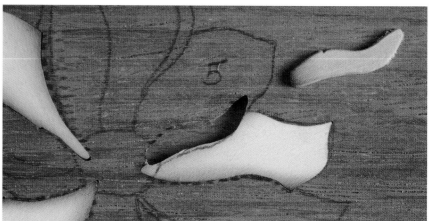

Only the end of the maple insert piece gets shaded, so it will appear to be behind the center of the flower.

The shading looks consistent with the other shaded pieces.

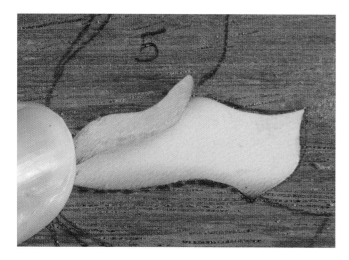

Glued in place, the subtle color difference between the maple and holly is apparent.

Transfer the missing pattern line to continue with petal #5.

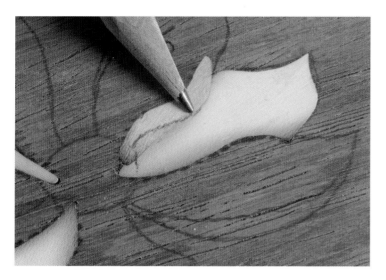

This point is important to helping the underside of the maple petal look believable. The transition from holly to maple on petal #5 needs to be fluid and natural, just as we see in nature.

Again, I'll overlap into petal #6 as well as the flower's center.

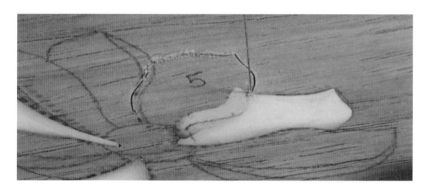

I've completed sawing the top of the petal and now the saw blade is approaching the maple underside. This is the transition that is important in making the petal look natural. Essentially, I need to leave a very fine point on the maple insert piece. This helps the eye move easily over the finished petal rather than creating an awkward imperfection that draws the eye to this point.

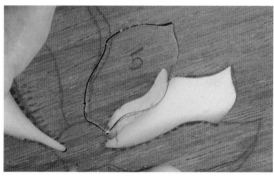

Here is another view of the transition, before lifting out the waste piece. Notice on the lower right side where the saw kerf contacts the maple insert piece. By aiming the blade carefully as I approach the maple, I've left a very fine point, which helps the petal look more natural.

I'll concentrate the shading for piece #5 along this edge.

The piece is nicely shaded without looking charred.

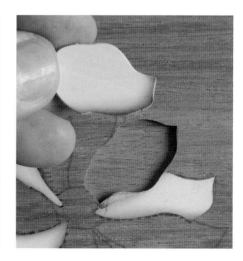

Piece #5 is also shaded near the center of the flower.

Petal #5 is glued in place. Notice the fit of petal #1 compared to the other pieces—it's slightly loose along the shaded area because the hot sand shrank it. The slight adjustment I made to the sawing angle on the following pieces has left a tight fit after shading. I mention this as a way of reinforcing the importance of reviewing the results of the fit and making small changes as necessary. Consistency leads to fluid, satisfying work. The gaps on petal #1 will eventually be cut away with future insert pieces, leaving the final marquetry image clean and tight.

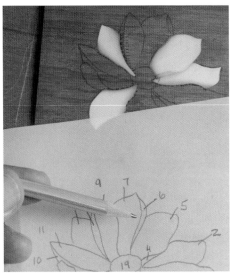

Petal #6 is the underside of petal #7, also maple.

The red dotted sawing line overlaps into the next petal.

Beginning the cut.

After turning the corner at the point of the cut, I saw back toward the center.

Returning to the drill hole after cutting into the center of the flower slightly.

The maple insert piece is ready for shading.

Again, just the tip, which sits at the center of the flower gets shaded.

Checking that the shading is similar to the previous pieces.

Gluing the piece into place.

The shading looks pretty consistent to this point.

Here is the drill hole location for petal #7.

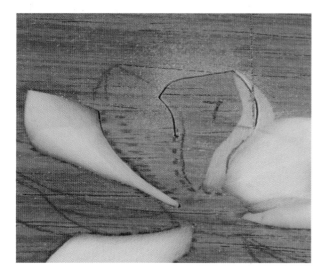

Half way through the cut, I am removing most of the maple from petal #6.

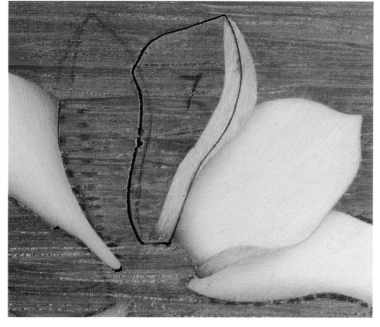

Before removing the waste piece, it's easy to see the path of the blade. There are sharp points at both ends of the maple insert piece, which help it to look like it is the underside of the petal. It seems I didn't need to shade petal #6 at the center of the flower!

Shaded and glued in place. I'm holding my finger on the outline of the flower's center to help visualize the final shading of these three finished petals. The shading looks consistent and is beginning to give the design a three-dimensional feel.

Now I skip over to maple piece # 8. I've drawn this pencil line by hand rather than using the pattern. That way I have a little more control over the amount of shading that will remain from petal #1. Notice that the gap I mentioned early is about to be cut away. The drill hole for this cut will be in petal #9.

Threading the blade through the veneers.

After turning the corner at the flower center, I cut a nice, fair curve along the pencil line.

Cutting back to the beginning.

Here is the waste piece. Notice the thin amount of holly from petal #1 along with the gap.

I'm shading just the end of the maple insert piece, where it will contact the center of the flower.

With petal #8 glued in place, I'm ready to work on #9. The holly is taped to the narra background veneer with the holly grain orientation running with the length of the petal. I've used the pattern and graphite paper to replace the missing pencil lines. This petal is surrounded by other finished pieces, so I'll put the drill hole in the flower center where it will be cut away at the end of the project.

Reaching the top of the petal, I push my sawing hand forward a little and begin pivoting around the corner.

Now cut a nice, long curve along the shaded holly.

With the piece shaded and glued in place, I'm using a small scraper to lightly remove glue and pencil lines so I can take a look at the marquetry image.

Progress. The shading looks consistent, as does the fit of the individual pieces. It's beginning to look like a flower.

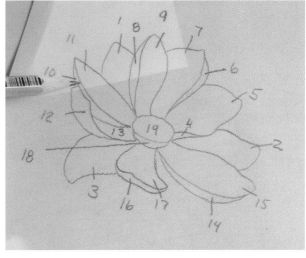

Piece #10 will be a maple piece that's hiding behind a couple of others, so it goes in next.

The red dotted line shows that the piece overlaps everywhere except the top of the petal, furthest from the flower center.

I'll drill in the adjacent piece.

Once I leave the neighboring petal, I saw directly on the pencil line to the outer point.

Carefully turn the corner and back along the red dotted line, near the pencil line.

Then, cut into the center of the flower.

Now, back to the beginning.

Retransfer all of the lines that were cut away.

We need to add shadow right here to make the next petal look like it's on top of this one.

Shade that small area.

Also shade near the center of the flower.

Piece #10 is glued in place.

Retransfer the line that was cut away.

I've redrawn the line and indicated the sequence of upcoming cuts.

I carefully align the holly veneer so I don't cut into a void.

The drill hole location is near petal #11 in the flower's center.

Here again is the slightly angled position of the saw to tighten the fit.

I am cutting just inside the edge of the holly to preserve some of the shading.

Test fit.

Shading along one edge and then the end near the flower's center.

Holding the shaded piece above the background veneer confirms the shading looks consistent.

Petal #12 is next. This piece only overlaps a little into piece #13. The drill hole will go here on the red dotted line.

This part of the design brings up a question as to which piece (#12 or #13) gets cut first. With every marquetry piece, I'm trying not to paint myself into a corner, where I would face a very difficult cut or have a result that is not as sharp, too thin, or not properly located. This is why the sequence of cuts is so important.

In this case, both #12 and #13 have very fine, pointed corners. Whichever piece gets cut first can overlap into the other, so it becomes an easier piece to make. The following piece is often a little more difficult because (as in this situation) a very sharp corner has to be made.

In this example, choosing either #12 or #13 first leaves a cut that is similar in difficulty. So I've chosen to go with the one on the left (#12) first because at least I can easily hide both drill holes—the drill hole for #13 gets hidden in the center of the flower.

The beginning of the cut.

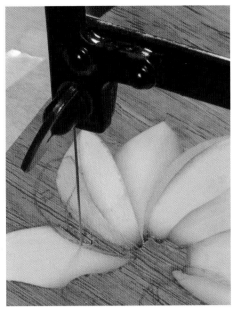

I've sawn past the corner on #12 and now I'm returning along the pencil line.

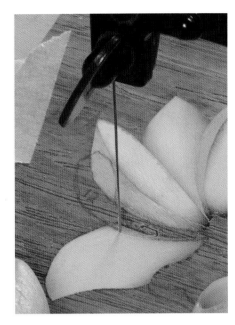

Exiting the holly, moving into the narra.

Approaching the outer corner of the petal.

Following the line into the maple.

Once I cross into piece #13, I move away from the line a little and back to the drill hole.

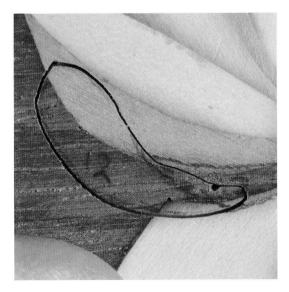

Before removing the waste piece, the path of the cut is clear.

The maple insert piece is temporarily in place. I'll shade this area a little to help it stand out from the maple behind it. Just a little will be enough.

The shaded maple piece is glued in place. I've hand drawn this pencil line for piece #13 so that I get a smooth transition from the underside of the petal to the topside.

As mentioned earlier, the drill hole goes in the flower center.

Sawing along the holly, preserving some sand shading.

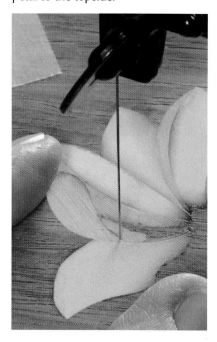

Cutting smoothly into the maple.

As I approach the corner, I move my sawing hand forward a little to help create a sharp corner.

Turning the corner and cutting smoothly back to the center of the flower.

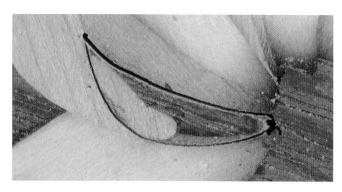

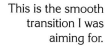

Viewing the path of the saw blade before removing the waste piece.

This is the smooth transition I was aiming for.

Only the end of the holly petal gets shaded.

Glued into place. The sharp corners and smooth transitions help make the image a little more believable.

Next is petal #14, a maple underside.

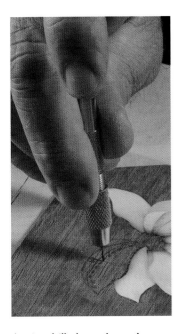

Again, drill along the red dotted line that overlaps into the next petal.

Here I've sawn past the corner of #14 and turned to saw along the outer pencil line.

Completing the cut.

Gluing the piece in place after shading the end where the petal joins the center of the flower.

Redrawing the line for the next petal.

I hand draw the line where the next piece cuts along the previous holly petal to preserve the sand shading.

Again, when orienting the holly below the background veneer, be careful to avoid any areas that have already been cut out of the holly.

Like the other pieces that are surrounded by completed petals, locate the drill hole in the center of the flower. Now I'm sawing the previously shaded holly piece.

Turning the outer corner and cutting back along the maple, I leave a fine point at both ends.

With the insert and waste removed, it's clear that you can create a very fine point by first inserting one piece and then cutting most of it away with a following piece.

After finishing the cut I loosen the blade.

Shading the end and along the edge where the holly touches the maple.

Applying glue to the edge of piece #15.

Next is the outer, maple underside of the last petal.

The maple veneer taped to the background veneer.

I won't need to shade this piece, so I can drill a little farther away than usual. This will give me room to make the corners wide.

I've taken a wide turn to lead into the shape of this piece.

Gluing piece #16 in place without shading.

This long oval shape gives me a lot of room for the long, sharp corners, which will be created when cutting the next petal.

With the lines redrawn, it's easy to see why we needed a lot of maple for the two sharp corners.

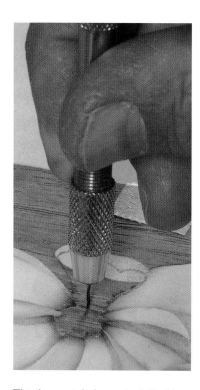

This last petal also gets drilled in the flower's center.

As I'm approaching the pencil line drawn on the maple, I'm aiming carefully at the edge of the maple, which will help me create a very fine point. Similarly, once I'm in the maple, I anticipate where to begin making the turn to exit the maple and leave a very fine point on the petal. Fine points help create the petal's three-dimensional appearance.

I've shaded the holly where it joins the flower center and where it touches the maple on the outer edge. Then I apply the glue.

Pressing piece #17 into place and tapping if necessary.

The shading looks consistent and the maple on the outer edge of petal #17 looks cup-shaped.

I've redrawn the center of the flower by hand. This way I can make the center a little larger or smaller depending on how much petal shading I want to leave around the center.

Initially I was going to use birch for the flower center (*far left*). Now that I see the finished petals, I think the birch might look too similar to the shaded areas around the center. So I would like to consider some other colors and textures.

The flower's center will be made from two pieces. The first piece will suggest the edge of the center and the second will be the face of the center of the flower. I'll use the dark area from the red gum *(right)* for the edge and sycamore *(top)* for the face of the flower.

I've oriented the center of the flower over the dark stripes on the red gum veneer.

Taping the red gum in place.

I'm drilling in the face of the flower, roughly in the center.

The shape of this piece is very similar to the last maple piece.

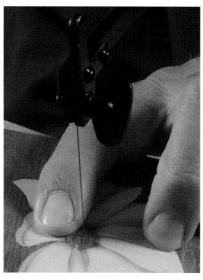

After sawing around the bottom of the shape, I'm returning to the center.

Completing the cut.

Redrawing the face of the flower center.

This is what the shape of the flower center will look like, leaving a nice amount of shading on the petals but removing the darkest shading and the drill holes.

I've chosen this area on the sycamore veneer for it's tight ray pattern.

Carefully locating the background veneer over the pattern I've chosen and taping it in place.

I'll drill the hole right here. This is the only time in the pattern when I can't hide the hole with a subsequent piece of marquetry. In this case, I prefer to locate the hole in a darker piece of wood—the red gum I just inserted.

The trick to hiding the hole is to drill a little steeper than usual, so that the top and bottom hole are in the waste piece.

Threading the blade through the veneers.

Sawing around the shape.

Gluing the sycamore piece into the center of the flower.

Here is the completed marquetry design. The shading looks consistent and the features appear to have depth.

With the marquetry complete, the veneers are ready to be glued to a core, which will be made up of two pieces of 1/8" plywood. I've identified the grain direction on the Baltic birch plywood. The plywood grain direction will be glued opposite of the veneer grain direction.

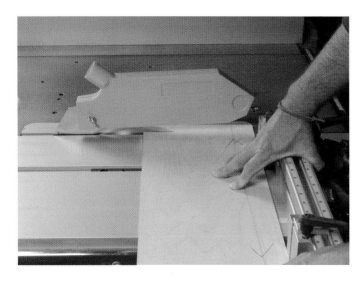

I start by squaring one end of the plywood on the table saw. My hands are positioned far away from the blade.

Laying the marquetry veneer on the plywood, with opposing grain direction, I mark the plywood slightly oversize.

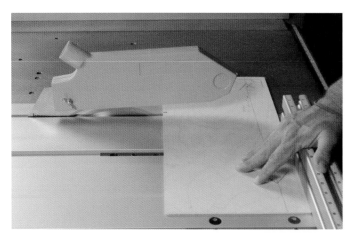

And cut on that line.

With that cut off piece, I mark the second piece of plywood.

Line the pencil mark up with the blade and cut. Both pieces of plywood are now slightly oversized.

Now I set the stop on the cut-off fence to the width of the marquetry veneer.

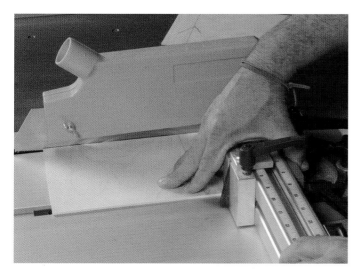

With the safety guard in position, I crosscut both pieces of plywood.

Then I reset the stop to the length of the marquetry veneer.

And rip the plywood to the veneer length

Veneers and plywood cut to size in preparation for glue-up.

Using a piece of MDF with a thin cleat attached to one end, I scrape the back of the marquetry veneer flat.

Once flat, the backside can be sanded or left as a scraped surface.

I scrape the front of the veneer and then sand it smooth with 220-grit sand paper. The scraper has left the surface very flat and pretty smooth, so I don't need to use sandpaper coarser than 220 at this stage. After the panel is glued to the core, I'll sand again with 220-, then 320-, and finish with 400-grit paper.

The veneers and plywood are ready for the glue-up. I've identified the glue side of both veneers.

I assemble the pieces and draw my cabinetmaker's triangle on one edge.

As with the practice panel glue-up earlier, these are the supplies I use to glue up small panels.

I fold the corners on a few pieces of tape and stick them to the front of the marquetry veneer.

Using a plastic glue spreader, I apply an even amount of yellow or white woodworking glue to the first piece of plywood.

I repeat with both sides of each piece of plywood and finally the back veneer. I stretch the tape tight to keep the pieces from sliding on the wet glue.

Placing kraft paper or newspapers on both sides of the project protect it from becoming glued to the MDF.

The small work piece needs four clamps, spaced evenly.

While the top panel is drying, I'll jump to the bottom panel of the box. I've prepared the pieces just as I did the top panel. The only difference is this panel will be thinner, so I'll only use one piece of 1/8" plywood. Notice the grain orientation. I'm making the bottom panel now because I'll need to know it's final thickness when I'm constructing the sides for the box.

Again, fold the corners of a few pieces of tape and place on one of the veneer surfaces.

Apply glue evenly to both sides of the plywood.

And wrap the tape tightly around the panel.

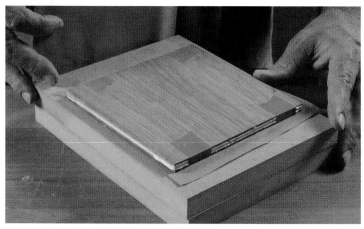

Again, sandwich the panel between paper.

And tighten with clamps

After a couple of hours I unclamp the bottom panel and set it aside until it's needed. I'm careful not to place the panel flat on the workbench after it is unclamped, as this will likely cause the panel to warp. Instead I stand it upright or clamp it in a vise to allow the moisture from the glue to evaporate evenly from both surfaces.

Assembling the Box

With the top and bottom panels glued up, I'll turn my attention to the box itself. Here is the piece of narra that will make the sides of the box. As I mentioned earlier, I'll be choosing the box sides from the straighter grain on the nearer side of the board.

STRAIGHTENING the wood grain for a woodworking project is a very easy thing to do and always worthwhile. To my eye, it helps the finished piece have a balanced feel. And it helps draw the eye to the part of the piece where the attention belongs—the marquetry top. Carelessly chosen wood grain can compete with the design of a box or furniture piece.

TIP

The grain is slashed a little, running uphill to the right. I've placed a straight stick near the middle of the board, lined up with the grain. This helps me visualize the part of the board I'll use for the box sides. In other words, I can use any part of the board as my reference or starting point for straight grain. I don't have to use one of the edges from the sawmill, which in this case, are not parallel to the grain.

The box sides are 2 1/4" wide. Here I'm holding a ruler at 2 1/2" from the near edge of the board. I'm starting on the left because the grain runs uphill on the right side of the wood. If I start here, I'll be sure to have more than enough width for the box sides. I make a pencil mark here.

Then I position my straight stick on that pencil mark and align the stick with the grain. Once I'm certain the stick and the grain are parallel to each other, I draw a pencil line the length of the board. Notice the grain pattern on the far right side of the board is curving away from the straight section. That end will eventually be cut off, as the board is a few inches too long.

The pencil line will become the board's new straight edge.

At the band saw, rip nice and straight along the pencil line.

Here is the new edge of the board. I'll joint this rough edge on the jointer.

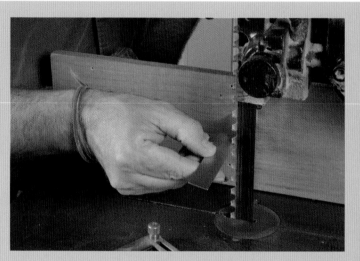

I want my finished side to be 2 1/4" wide, so I'll set the band saw fence about 1/16" more than that. I'll use the thickness planer to plane down to the final width.

With the newly jointed edge against the fence, I rip the board to the oversized width.

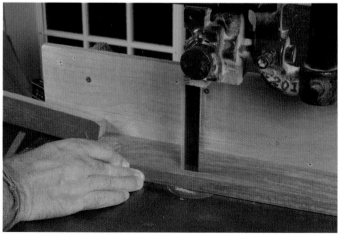

Finishing the cut with a push stick.

I like these fingers, so I keep them clear of the blade as I near the end of the cut.

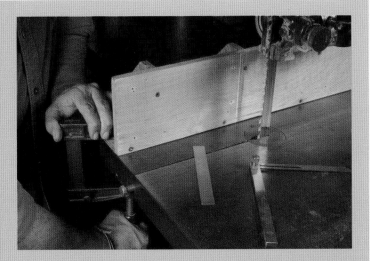

I've double-checked the drift of the blade with the previously set bevel square and clamped the fence tight.

The straightened edge of the board. The swirling grain on the far left will be cut away later.

This is my small Inca jointer/planer. It's a little small for some of the furniture I make, but very accurate and ideal for this project.

At the jointer, I determine the grain direction of the narra and take a light pass, cutting with the grain, to produce a flat face. Make a mark of some kind on the newly jointed face to indicate it's now flat.

With the newly jointed face against the fence, joint one edge.

I've made a mark on the edge indicating this edge has been jointed and is now the new reference edge.

My Inca jointer/planer is a combination machine. Here I've removed the jointer outfeed table so that I can thickness plane the width to 2 1/4" wide.

The planer cuts very cleanly and leaves only a very small amount of snipe (a slightly deeper cut) at the beginning and end of the board, which is the reason I left the board long to begin with. This way I can remove the snipe when I cut the board to its final length.

With one face and one edge milled flat, I'm ready to re-saw the narra in half. The narra is a little less than 7/8" thick, so I'll re-saw and end up with two pieces that are less than 3/8" thick. I want the box sides to be 1/4" or a little more in final thickness. I work this way so that my grain will be consistent, with the pattern wrapping around the box.

I adjust the fence so that I'm re-sawing just about in the center of the board. The fence is also adjusted for the blade drift.

After I've clamped the fence in place, I check to be sure I have enough thickness for the eventual 1/4" box sides. Here my ruler reads about 5/16". That leaves enough thickness to re-joint and thickness plane the wood after I re-saw the pieces.

Begin re-sawing with the jointed face firmly against the fence.

I complete the re-saw pass with the push stick.

Moving back to the jointer, I joint a new face on *both* pieces. Even though I previously jointed one face, the board has almost certainly bowed a little as tension was released when re-sawing. At this stage I always assume nothing is flat.

After both pieces are jointed I thickness plane down to the final thickness of 1/4".

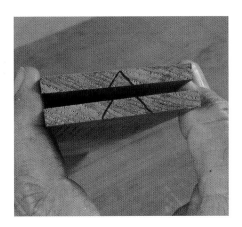

Here are the 1/4" thick sides with cabinetmaker's triangle. This triangle is important for the next few steps.

The box will have mitered corners, so at this stage I'll cut the front, back, and sides a little longer than necessary.

I want the grain pattern to wrap around the box, so rather than casually choosing the four sides, I lay out the cuts like this. I'm working from the right side because I want to cut off the swirling grain on the left.

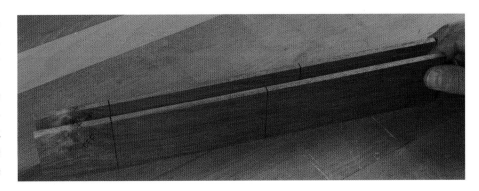

I've drawn pencil lines that layout how the box parts are being chosen. Starting with the section my thumb is on and moving clockwise, the marked sections are as follows: front side, left side, back side, and right side. Arranging the pieces this way will allow the grain pattern to wrap around the box.

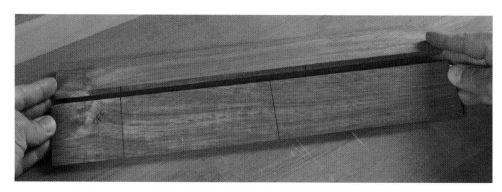

As I fold the 2 pieces down, the surfaces that were the outside of the board before it was re-sawn will be the exterior surfaces of the box.

I put blue tape on the upward facing faces, with the tape hanging over the edges of the boards. These indicate the top edge of the box sides and the exterior surfaces of the box sides.

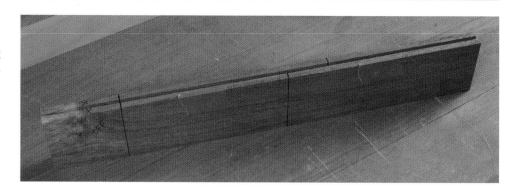

With the pieces standing again, the tape is visible on the top edges.

Now I label the tape. Front and left on the near board. Back and right on the far board. The longer section on the far board is obviously the back.

I fold the tape over the top edge so that it's clear which is the top when I am working at the machines.

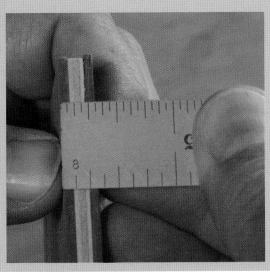

Before I cut the sides shorter, I want to cut a dado, or groove, on the interior of all the box sides for the bottom panel. With the bottom panel already prepared, I've scraped and sanded it to final thickness so that I can measure its final dimension, which is 5/16" thick.

I've put a small dado set in the sliding table saw and I've adjusted the height to a little less than 1/8". This will cut less than halfway through the thickness of the box sides.

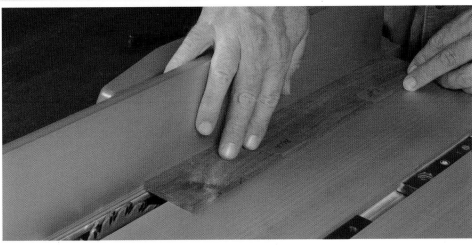

And now, the reason for the blue tape on the face and top edge of the sides is clear. If I have the board placed correctly on the table saw, I should be able to see the tape. If the tape is against the fence, it should raise an alarm that something is wrong. Only the wood should be touching the fence and the tape should be easily seen. I'm adjusting the fence so that the blade is about 5/16" away and locked in position.

With the fence locked, I use a push stick to make the cut. The black push stick is helping hold the board against the fence. It does not travel forward with the board. I only want to apply side pressure in front of the blade.

Completing the cut.

Both pieces have a clean 5/16" wide groove.

Now I'll crosscut on the pencil lines to make the pieces closer to size.

To cut the mitered corners, tilt the table saw blade to 45 degrees.

With the pieces closer to the final size, I cut a 45-degree angle on the end of each piece.

For the smaller pieces I'll use a clamp device to keep my hands far from the blade.

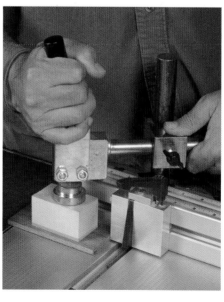

The piece is clamped in position.

Making the 45-degree cut.

To test the 45-degree angle for accuracy, I hold two pieces tight against a square and check that the angle fits perfectly. If the fit is not tight, I still have enough room to make an adjustment to the saw and test again. Here the angle looks very good.

Measuring the final length from the mitered cut and making a pencil mark.

Leave the saw set up for mitering, move the stop into place, and lock it in position.

And make the cut.

Now I repeat the process for the left and right side of the box. Measure to length.

Adjust the stop and clamp the piece into position.

And cut the remaining miters.

With the miters cut, I can remove the blue tape.

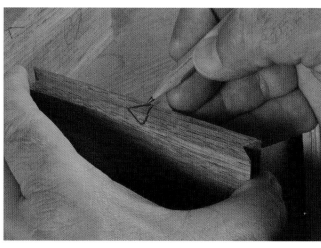

I hold the sides together and mark a cabinetmaker's triangle across both pieces.

With the front and back held together, draw the same triangle again. The base of the triangle rests on the front of the box.

The triangle helps me to always know which piece goes in which position.

Now I carefully sand the inside surfaces with 220- and 320-grit sandpaper.

Soften the bottom inside edge a little to make it friendlier to the touch. The bottom inside edge is difficult to sand after the box is glued together because the bottom panel is so close.

I've applied a little shellac to the fad and I'm putting a few coats on the interior of the box parts. On the ends pieces, I'll shellac the entire surface.

On the front and back (the longer pieces), however, I only shellac the narrow surface beside the groove and about 1/2" along the top of the panel. I do this because I plan on gluing a divider in the box later, so I need to leave most of the surface as raw wood so the glue will bond. I'll build up a few coats on these narrow strips.

The finished surfaces. I also wax these same areas at this time. The wax will make it easier to clean up any glue that gets squeezed out later.

These four pieces of thick cardboard will protect the corners during the glue-up. The pieces are about 2 1/4" x 1 1/2".

Cut the cardboard with a knife.

Score lengthwise down the center.

When folded, the cardboard will prevent the corners from being damaged.

I'll use two band clamps to glue up the box.

With the box squeezed tight without glue, I'll measure for the bottom panel.

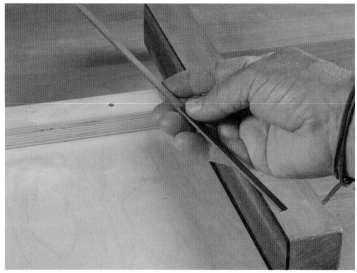

In order to measure a captured distance like the bottom panel, I'll make story sticks. I'll use a long strip of sawn veneer about 1/16" x 1/2".

First, square one end of the story stick. I'll use a shop-made shooting board. This is just a flat and square board made of two layers of 1/2" birch plywood with a shelf for a long plane and a cleat. The cleat is very carefully positioned so that it is perfectly square with the bottom of the plane. The long plane travels toward the cleat. The story stick, or any piece of wood, is held tight against the cleat and gets planed perfectly square.

My left hand is holding the story stick and my right hand makes light passes until the stick is square.

With the square end of the story stick held tight in the bottom groove, I make a pencil mark indicating the approximate location of the opposite groove.

I use a small saw to cut a little longer than the pencil line.

Then I begin shooting (planing) to the line, staying a little long at first.

Flex the stick into the grooves.

It's easy to see the stick is still too long.

131

A little more shooting will fix that.

A perfect fit.

I make a second story stick for the width of the bottom panel. Now I have the exact dimensions of the bottom panel.

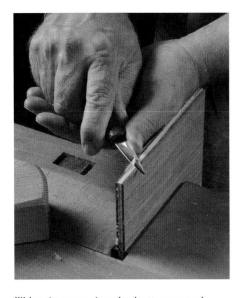

I'll begin preparing the bottom panel by cutting off any glue squeeze-out with a knife.

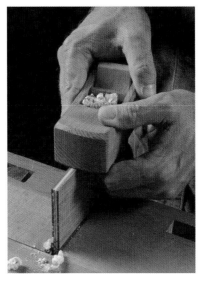

Then, plane one edge straight and square. This edge becomes the reference at the table saw.

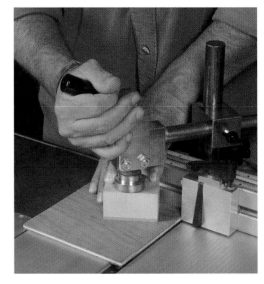

I clamp the bottom panel in position with the reference edge against the crosscut fence.

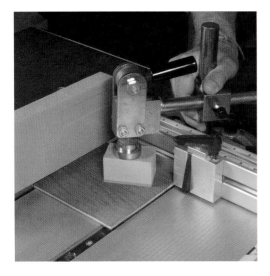

And cut one edge square to the first.

Then I use the long story stick to set the fence stop to the exact distance from the blade. The story stick eliminates the risk of making a mistake with a ruler. I'm actually setting the stop so the distance is a fraction less than the story stick—maybe 1/32" shorter. This way I prevent any possibility of the bottom panel preventing the miters from coming together perfectly in the box glue-up.

The clamp device keeps the panel secure during the cut.

Now I'll set the saw to the length of the shorter story stick. Again, I'll set the stop a fraction less than the length of the stick.

Double-checking my setting.

Making the last cut.

At the bench, I plane the bottom panel to make a perfect fit in the groove.

Test fit.

Once I'm happy with the fit, I ease the corners a little with the plane. This helps the panel get into the groove a little easier.

Test fit the bottom panel with the sides.

Checking that the miters close completely and the bottom panel doesn't rattle in the grooves.

Before putting a finish on the panel, I'll carve my initials on the bottom surface with a chip carving knife.

Pour a small amount of shellac on the fad.

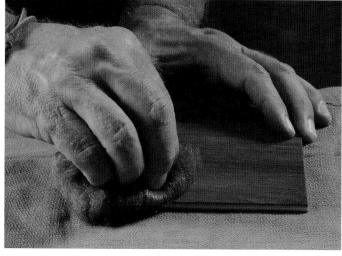

Shellac both sides of the panel with four or five coats to give the narra a nice sheen.

Rub the panel with #0000 steel wool between coats and after the last coat. Then, wax the bottom and steel wool it when the wax has dried.

Before gluing the box together, I make diagonal sticks. In this case, the diagonal sticks look a lot like story sticks because I've used the same scrap of veneer. Diagonal sticks measure the distance corner to corner and help produce a very square box.

Each stick is shorter than the corner-to-corner distance. Held together, however, they can be adjusted until they touch the corners.

Clamp the box together without glue. This is a dry run. The dry run helps assure I have everything on hand for the real glue-up and gets my mind focused.

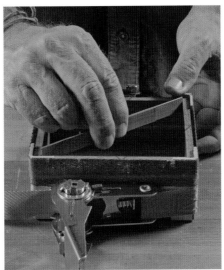

Without moving them, check the other direction. The box wants to square up nicely because the miters are truly at 45 degrees and the individual parts of the box are accurately sized. It's unusual to have to adjust squareness at this stage, but having the diagonal sticks ready takes away a little stress.

I slide the diagonal sticks to the opposite corners and pinch them together.

Here is a piece-by-piece view of the box with everything ready to go for the glue-up. I'll use a thick rubber band to hold the box together initially while the first clamp is positioned.

I use the accordion glue bottle to apply glue to all the miters. I'm applying a bead of glue a little outside the width of the miter so most of the squeeze-out moves outside the box.

The glue applied to all four corners.

I start by putting the bottom panel in the two sides and then I bring the front and back panels into position. This is my last chance to make sure my carved initials are on the bottom side of the box.

The pieces come together easily.

I put the cardboard corners and then the rubber band in place.

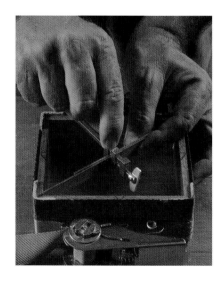

Tightening the first band clamp into position.

Then I place the second band clamp. Having band clamp pressure at the top and bottom of the box helps assure the corners come together.

Now that the box is gluing up, I return to the diagonal sticks, which are pressed into position. Once they are touching the opposite corners, I use a small clamp to keep this distance.

I double-check the opposite diagonal.

The finished box glue-up.

While the box is drying, I'll make new story sticks for the lid.

I shoot one end of the first stick square and then mark the location to cut.

Use the shooting board to trim the story stick to length.

The story stick indicates a nice, tight fit.

Repeat this process for the width of the lid, shooting it to the final size.

Test fit for the width.

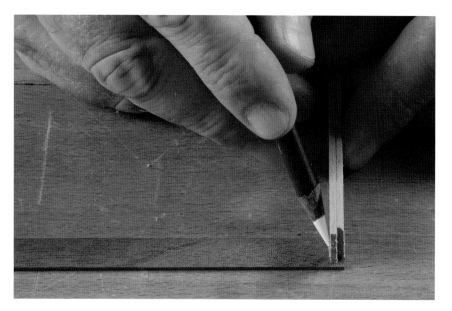

The story sticks represent the lid's overall dimensions. But I'll be applying an edge banding to the lid to cap the plywood core. So, to use the story sticks at the table saw, I need to take the thickness of the edge banding into account.

The edge banding will be made from strips of sawn veneer, just as I did on the practice marquetry panel. To use the table saw for cutting the box lid to its accurate size, I'll mark off the thickness of two pieces of edge banding on the story stick. Since my story sticks are walnut, I'll use a white colored pencil to make visible marks.

This is the distance I'll use to cut the length of the lid panel.

I repeat the same steps for the width.

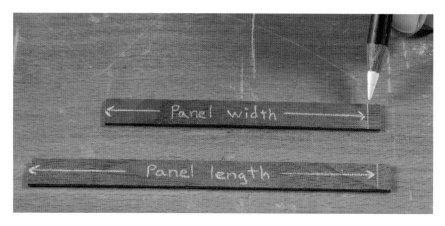

Now we have an accurate distance for length and width.

The veneer I used for the marquetry was quite a bit oversized. I use the story sticks to help decide where the image will be located on the final panel. I would like the design offset in the bottom left.

I've already planed this bottom edge of the lid panel, so that will be my reference edge. I make a pencil mark to represent my first table saw cut.

The pencil and the story sticks together help me visualize how the marquetry design will look in the end.

These two pencil marks indicate the bottom left corner of the lid.

I've already trimmed one end of the lid and now I'm using it as a reference against the fence. Here I'm preparing to cut the pencil line at the bottom of the marquetry design.

Making the cut with the work piece held firmly.

That bottom cut now becomes my reference. I want to cut on the pencil line I made with the story stick, but I need to see that line from the backside of the panel. Here I've transferred the mark around to the other side.

Setting the saw for that cut...

and cutting.

Setting the stop to cut precisely on the white story stick line. This is the length story stick.

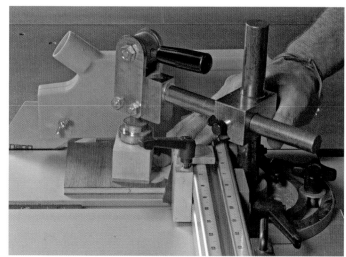

Cutting the panel to its final length.

Now, set the saw to cut the panel width, precisely to the line.

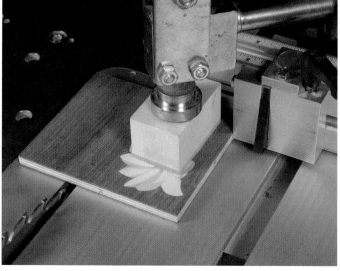

Clamped in place, the panel is prepared for its last cut.

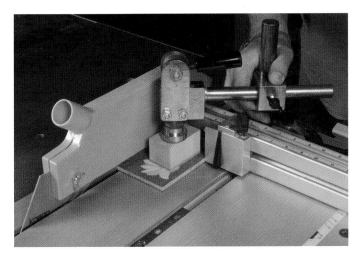

Moving the lid panel through the blade.

The lid panel cut to its final size.

With the box lid cut to size, I'll jump back to the box itself. I let the box dry for about four hours and then remove the clamps and cardboard corners.

I use a sharp hand plane to clean up and flatten the exterior of the box, being careful to plane with the grain direction. The box is small and is easily held in the tail vise.

Checking for smooth and flat surfaces.

The plane leaves a beautiful, iridescent finish and crisp corners. If you choose to sand the surface instead, use a flat sanding block beginning with 220-grit paper. Working up through 400-grit paper will leave a nice surface. Work carefully to keep the sides flat.

Now I flatten the bottom edges so the box sits nicely on the bench. Holding the box in the tail vise, I begin near one corner and travel completely around the bottom of the box. As always, the plane is set very fine and the blade is extremely sharp.

Turn the corner and plane one of the long edges.

Continuing around the next corner. An advantage to shop-made wooden planes is they can be pulled or pushed. Usually two or three times around the bottom will clean it up nicely and make a very flat surface.

The bottom of the box is flat and very crisp.

Now complete the same steps on the top of the box, making it perfect and smooth.

The finished edges on the top of the box are also clean and even.

At this stage I use a knife to release any dried glue from the inside corners. Because shellac and wax were already applied to the interior, the glue pops out very easily.

Next I want to make spline keys on the corners of the box. The keys give the glue joint a little more strength and a nice visual decoration. To make the cuts for the keys, I'll use this simple plywood jig.

The jig is used vertically. The box sits on the cleats while the band saw cuts a groove in the corner.

Here I use a 45-degree square to draw a line through the middle of the miter joint.

Then, measure the distance from the corner of the box to that pencil line. It measures 5/16".

Next I decide where I'd like the spline keys located. I've drawn pencil marks about 1/4" from the top and bottom of the box.

Now I use that 5/16" to draw a mark along the 1/4" mark. The 5/16" mark is the stopping point for the saw kerf. In other words, it is the depth of the cut.

The pencil is pointing to the depth of cut mark.

I set a combination square to 1/4" and mark around the top and bottom of the box.

Then I reset the combination square to 5/16" and mark the depth of the cut marks at the end of all the 1/4" marks.

This is what it looks like with the marks completed.

The jig is held against the band saw fence with the box sitting in the cleats. I clamp the fence in position so that the blade lines up with the 1/4" pencil marks.

A close-up of what I'm looking at

The saw kerf from my band saw blade is 1/16" thick. The strips of sawn veneer from my marquetry veneers fit snugly in the kerf. These strips are 1/2" wide.

I cut a handful of pieces about 3/4" long.

Apply glue in a saw kerf.

Now, press the spline into place, making sure it goes all the way to the bottom of the kerf.

Turn on the saw and slide the jig and box together into the blade and cut to the 5/16" depth of cut mark.

Rotate the box and repeat the cut.

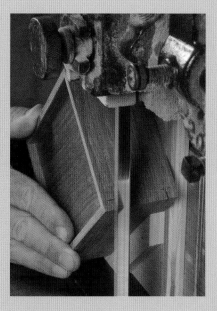

Once all the kerfs have been cut at the top of the box, I flip the box over and cut the bottom corners.

All eight splines are in place.

145

While the splines are drying, I edge band the top panel using the same method I used on the earlier practice panel. The edge banding is cut a little wider and longer than the actual edge of the panel. Apply glue and use blue tape as the clamp.

When the glue has dried for about 30 minutes, I use a hand plane to bring the edge banding nearly flush with the panel.

Then I use the wood file to make it flush. Repeat on the other overhangs.

To cut the edge banding to length, I put two pieces of blue tape on the edge of the panel and use a flush-cut saw to cut the excess wood.

Then, use the file to make the edge band perfectly flush with the panel.

Apply glue to the adjacent edges.

Tape the last two pieces of edge band in place.

146

Once dry, the hand plane cleans up the edge band and the file makes them completely flush.

Two pieces of tape shim the flush-cut saw. Then file the last corners flush.

Next I use 220-grit sand paper to make the marquetry panel smooth and remove any marks from the machines.

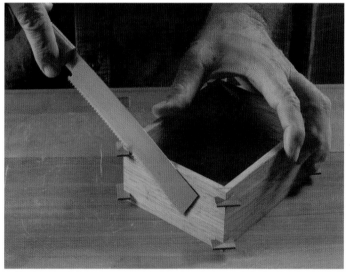

Returning to the box, I use the flush-cut saw to cut off the dried splines.

With the excess cut off, the file makes the spline keys flush.

Finally, I use the sharp hand plane to make the sides perfectly true again. The plane is set very fine so I'm only making a very light cut.

The box is nearly finished. The spline keys compliment the color and texture of the box while giving the miter joint a little more strength.

Now I need to make two dividers for the box interior. The box lid will rest on these dividers. I use the band saw to re-saw the remaining narra into 1/8" pieces. Usually, I saw a little thick and then use the drum sander to thickness sand to 1/8" thick. A thickness planer could also be used to arrive at 1/8". But if your saw is adjusted carefully it could produce pieces that are 1/8".

Now that the box has a bottom panel, the depth of the box is 1 3/4". I want the dividers to be a little below the top of the box, so that the lid sits inside the box. I'll rip the divider pieces to 1 5/8" wide. With the saw turned off, I adjust the fence to 1 5/8".

I use a push stick to rip the dividers.

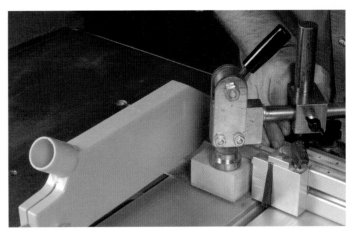

I set the table saw's crosscut stop using the same story sticks I used to cut the top panel to size. I set this distance a fraction longer than the story stick because I'll use the shooting board and long plane to fine-tune the dividers and make them fit perfectly.

Once the saw is set, crosscut the dividers to length.

The long shooting plane creates a perfectly square edge while gradually fitting the divider to the box.

The divider fits snugly inside the box.

Once the dividers fit, I ease the edges with the hand plane, making them a little friendlier to the touch.

Here are the softened edges of the dividers.

The dividers are in place, temporarily.

One surface and the long edges of each divider are finished. Here I'm building up shellac just as I did on the other box pieces. Four or five coats produce a nice sheen.

Before gluing the dividers in place, I ease the interior edges of the box. The bottom interior edges were softened before the glue up. Only the top needs to be done now.

A sanding block softens the long edges of the exterior. I'm using 320-grit paper.

I give the corners of the box the same light sanding.

Now I can glue the dividers into place.

Spring clamps and pads hold the dividers tightly against the sides of the box.

After drying about an hour, I remove the spring clamps and fit the lid to the box. With the edge bandings in place, the lid is just a fraction too tight to fit in the box. I use the shooting board and long plane, set very fine, to shoot or trim the lid to fit. It only needs a couple passes on each edge. This also makes the edges very smooth.

The lid fits tightly with just enough play to be removed easily.

Soften the lid's edges and corners with 320-grit sand paper and a sanding block.

Now the lid and box are ready for shellac.

I apply shellac to the lid surface, gradually building up a nice finish. As always, the fad is held tight in a ball shape. The shellac really makes the marquetry pop.

Shellac the edges as well.

While the first coats are drying on the lid, I shellac the edges of the box. Only add a small amount of shellac to the fad.

Now I shellac the sides of the box. Four or five coats of shellac give narra wonderful sheen. As always, I use steel wool between coats, making the shellac a little more even and smooth. Once this coat is drying, I'll shellac the bottom edges.

After the last coat of shellac, I use steel wool on all surfaces.

Then sweep the steel wool dust away
and apply wax to the box and lid.

Waxing the last surfaces. Once the wax dries
in five to ten minutes, I use steel wool to
remove any excess and dust each part.

Here is the finished marquetry box.

I think a simple box is a nice piece to showcase a marquetry project. Each project like this is an opportunity to grow as a woodworker and develop new skills. As in life, a job well done is very satisfying and something to be very proud of.

I encourage you to practice and continue developing your hand skills, which open the door to imagination.

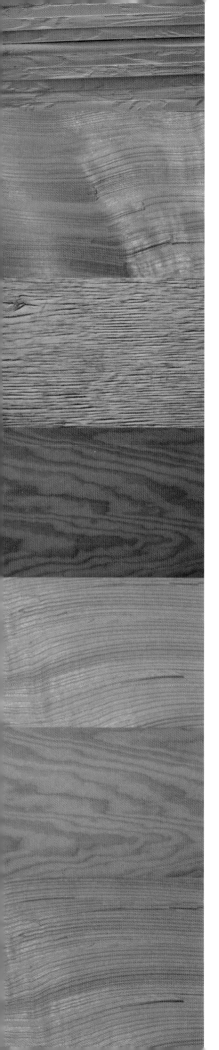

RESOURCES

Craig Vandall Stevens

In addition to offering small or one-on-one workshops in his own studio, Craig also sells packets of sawn veneers for folks that don't have the equipment or time to make their own. Contact him if you need an assortment of veneers to get started or would like to add to your supply of colors and textures.

craig@cvstevens.com
www.cvstevens.com

Marquetry Tools & Supplies

A & M Wood Specialty Inc.
358 Eagle St.
PO Box 32040
Cambridge, Ontario N3H 5M2
Canada
1-519-653-9322
1-800-265-2759 (US)
www.forloversofwood.com

• Wide variety of high-grade solid wood and veneers

Clapham's Beeswax Products
324 LeFeuvre Rd.
Abbotsford, BC V4X 1A2
Canada
1-604-856-2085

• Wax finish

Frei and Borel
126 2nd St.
Oakland, California 94607
1-800-772-3456
www.ofrei.com

• Saw blades for marquetry (2/0 jeweler's blades)
   • Item # 149.406 (1 dozen)
   • Item #149.406G (1 Gross)

• Pin vise: item # 58.220

Hearne Hardwoods
200 Whiteside Dr.
Oxford, PA 19363
1-888- 814-0007
fax: 610-932-3130
hearnehardwoods@chesco.com

• High-grade hardwoods

Highland Hardware
1045 N. Highland Ave., NE
Atlanta, GA 30306
1-800-241-6748
www.highlandwoodworking.com

• 11" Eclipse brand fret saw: item #451903

MSC Industrial Supply Co
www.mscdirect.com
1-800-645-7270

• #69 drill bits: item #01188697

Slidewright
1-877-754-3397
www.slidewright.com

• Sandvik Oberg files

Stewart - MacDonald's Guitar Shop Supply
21 N. Shafer St.
Box 900
Athens, Ohio 45701
1-800-848-2273
www.stewmac.com

• Abalone shell
• Inlay supplies and tools

Woodcraft Supply
1-800-225-1153
www.woodcraft.com

• Scrapers
• Sharpening stones
• Shellac flakes
• Other high quality woodworking supplies

Donkey

PATTERNS

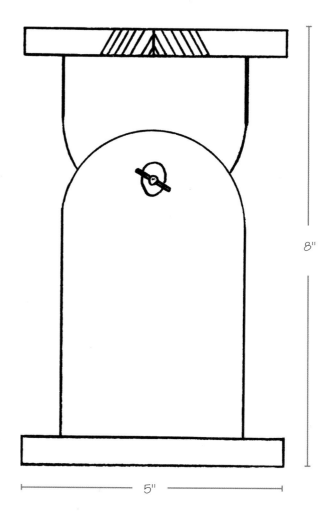

8"

5"

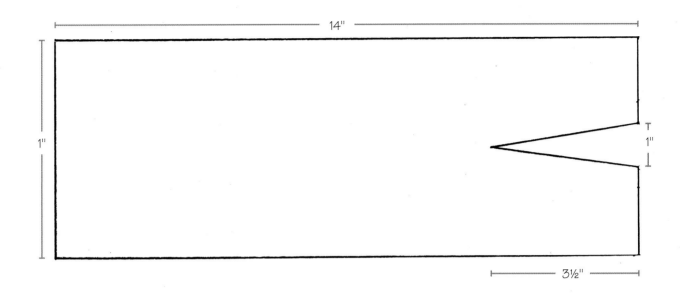

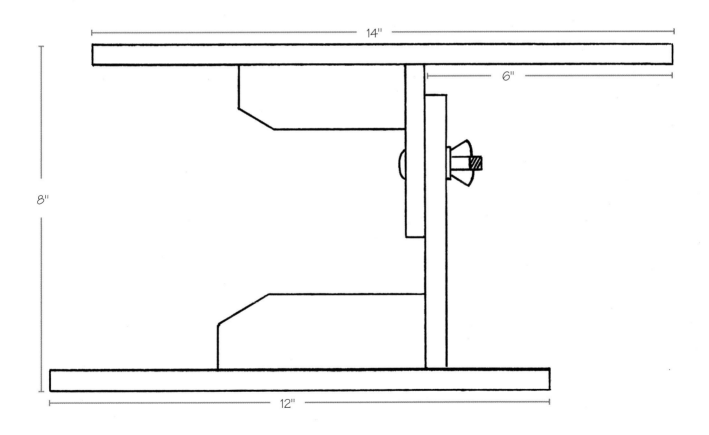

Leaf Pattern

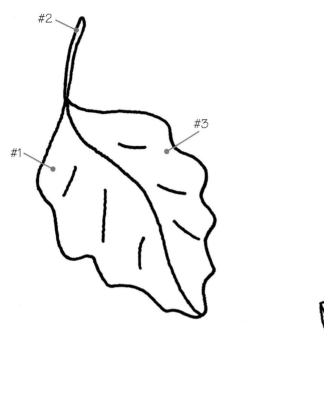

Lotus Pattern

Lotus with Cut Sequence

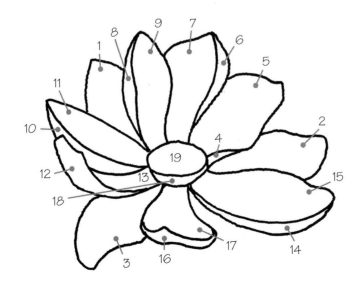